To Lisa
Our k...

from

Jasper and Ebony.
xx   xx

9th July 1992.

£10.

Withdrawn

2

29

A PASSION FOR
Dogs

A PASSION FOR Dogs

THE DOGS HOME BATTERSEA

Forewords
by Katie Boyle and Desmond Morris

Introduction
by HRH Prince Michael of Kent

David & Charles

Frontispiece:
Dog and man – a relationship that
has stood the test of time

British Library Cataloguing in Publication Data

A passion for dogs.
  1. Livestock. Dogs
  I. Battersea Dogs Home
  636.7

  ISBN 0-7153-9409-6 H/B
  ISBN 0-7153-0071-7 P/B

First published 1990
Second impression 1991
First published in paperback 1992

Typeset and designed by John Youé
on a Macintosh system
and printed in Italy
by OFSA SpA
for David & Charles Publishers
Brunel House   Newton Abbot   Devon

Contents

Foreword

by Katie Boyle

Travel abroad anywhere and the chances are that someone along the line, probably when you're stroking a four-legged foreigner, will say 'Oh, you come from Britain. Everyone treats dogs like members of the family in that country. . . '!

But do they? Not if the following figures are anything to go by.

In just one year the total of dogs taken in at The Dogs Home Battersea increased from 20,000 to 22,000 odd. A staggering number, made up of twenty-two thousand individual and miserably bewildered animals. To make matters worse, this annual total is still rising, and animal welfare associations all over the country can tell similar stories of overflowing premises.

As a longstanding and very active member of Battersea Dogs Home Committee, I see many of these creatures myself, and can assure you that it is always a heartrending experience. Dogs are abandoned on motorways, tied to railings, left at railway stations, collected from police kennels or simply handed over to strangers

The Dogs Home Battersea

(Gifts to the Home we call these at Battersea), often because they have become old and infirm, so their owners want to exchange them for a new model or just can't be bothered with them anymore.

I'm not talking simply of mongrels in their infinite varieties — far from it. Look down our lists and you'll see breed names which would do credit to Crufts. But you probably wouldn't recognise these purebreds by the time they reach us.

The confidence of the German Shepherd, the dignity of the Great Dane, the spirit of the terriers and the pride of the Pekes are all sadly and badly dented by the cruelty and irresponsibility of man.

Luckily, we do find some wonderful homes for our orphans, and for as long as I can remember my own family of dogs has always consisted of rescuees. To my mind, there are few more rewarding experiences than to see the fear and apprehension in the eyes of a previously ill-treated dog, gradually turn to an expression of total trust; and it's such fun to share games with dogs who have never 'laughed' before in their lives.

Thank God there are still many people who thoroughly enjoy the fun, the companionship, the unquestioning devotion and loyalty that a relationship with a dog can bring.

All of *US* are going to love this imaginatively compiled book. But should these pages tempt the previously 'unconverted' to get a pooch, do bear in mind that a dog is a daily commitment for many years, so please resist a passing temptation (as well as children's pleas) to experiment half-heartedly with dog owning. It would be cruel to add to our Battersea Annual Statistics.

The proceeds of this book will be donated to The Battersea Dogs Home. How wonderful! Thank you for buying it and for thus helping to improve the fate of potentially the most rewarding of creatures — The Dog!

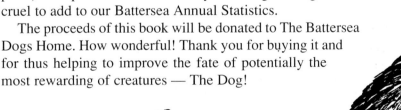

Foreword

by Desmond Morris

Anyone who visits The Dogs Home Battersea will become painfully aware of how many times human beings have betrayed the trust put in them by their dogs. A few of the animals may be there despite the best intentions of their owners, but they are in the minority. The majority have been abandoned. In every corner there lurks a pair of eyes seeking the bond of affection that has been lost. The expression is not reproachful, merely puzzled. What went wrong? How did the bond of mutual attachment fail? To a dog, this is a bewildering problem, for dogs are such sociable beings. Betrayal of their close

friends is not part of their way of life. So when a human abandons them or, worse still, actively persecutes them, they have no way of handling the situation.

Some sit quietly shocked in a silent heap staring out at the world. Others bark and bark, trying to raise the alarm; for something, it seems to them, is very wrong. Still others do their best to give friendship-signals to passing humans who might, despite everything, befriend them. If you care about dogs, be prepared to respond strongly to the scene at Battersea, or any other animal sanctuary in the country. And, if you can offer a new home to these betrayed dogs, please do so. They need all the help they can get. If you can't go that far, then do at least buy a copy of this book, because all the royalties from it will be going to support the work that these vital dogs' homes are doing.

The dog is man's oldest animal companion, with a close relationship going back at least 12,000 years. During that time we have nearly always benefited more than the dogs from the association. They have so often lost out, despite the fact that they have given their human companions a total loyalty that puts most of us to shame. No animal has served us better or in more varied ways. Dogs have protected our homes, warned us of dangers, helped us on the hunt, herded our flocks, kept us warm at night, guided our blind, comforted our sick, tracked down criminals, helped the police with their enquiries, sniffed out dangerous drugs, and above all provided us with loving companionship that comforts the lonely, de-stresses the stressed, and warms the hearts of even the most healthy and sociable of us. They deserve our care and attention. It is the least we can do for them.

Anyone who demeans them or persecutes them is my enemy. When you have read *A Passion for Dogs* I hope you will feel the same . . .

Desmond Morris

Introduction

by HRH Prince Michael of Kent

My family has taken a keen interest in the Dogs Home Battersea since 1879 when my great-grandfather, King Edward VII, then Prince of Wales, made a tour of it, accompanied by Queen Marie of the Belgians. Five years later Prince Leopold, Duke of Albany, youngest son of Queen Victoria, left Battersea at the end of his visit with a small terrier called Skippy which became an ardent friend of his year old daughter Princess Alice, later Countess of Athlone, who died in 1981.

HRH Prince Michael of Kent with his two Labradors. The Royal Family has taken a keen interest in The Dogs Home Battersea since 1879

After Prince Leopold's visit, Queen Victoria sent her Private Secretary, Sir Henry Ponsonby to view the establishment. As a result, Her Majesty first began to pay a generous annual subscription to the Home and then, in 1888, became Patron. That honour was to

be repeated in 1956 when Her Majesty Queen Elizabeth II agreed to take up the same appointment.

When I became President of the Home, I already held the Presidency of the Kennel Club. I have thus been able to view the canine world from both extremes – from the pedigree world at Crufts to the street-wise animals of Battersea.

Now, I would like to leave some urgent messages in the minds of anyone thinking of taking on a dog. Do not acquire one unless it can be correctly fed, housed and exercised – including when you are on holiday. Train your dog properly and keep it under control so that it does not become a nuisance to the neighbours or cause accidents. Make sure your dog has a means of identification so that if it does get lost it can be brought back to you as quickly as possible; the last thing your local dogs' home wants is one more unclaimed animal. Look after your dog's health, and have it regularly inoculated. Lastly, remember that it is your responsibility to ensure your dog does not have unwanted puppies. Unwanted puppies are a public menace. To prevent them you will need to take steps to have your dog spayed or neutered.

If you can keep these points in mind when you or your friends next go to buy a dog, you will be acting humanely towards the dog as well as doing a public service.

HRH Prince Michael of Kent
President
The Dogs Home Battersea

Some dogs lie in a silent heap, quietly shocked, staring out at the world

This Passion for Dogs

'The only creature faithful to the end'

More than 80,000 people visit The Dogs Home Battersea each year, and over five million have visited the Home since 1860, when it opened its doors to London's stray dogs. There are those who come to look for a new friend, offering a loving home to an unwanted dog or to a stray that has remained unclaimed. There are those who come out of curiosity just to have a look at the Home, to see what it is like and what is done there. Why is it then that these people flock to the Home in their thousands and what is the hold that the dog appears to have over man. What are these strong bonds that seem to have caused

their destinies to run together, establishing a relationship that has stood the test of time.

Adoring companions

To answer these questions, it is necessary to go back to primeval times, for the origins of our domesticated friend and ally are buried in antiquity. The dog was certainly the first carnivore ever to be domesticated, and, what is more, trained. When horses, goats and sheep were still running wild, dogs were sharing the caves that sheltered man. It is possible that man originally hunted dogs for food and then having cornered or captured a bitch in whelp or already with her pups, decided to rear them as stock.

Once taken into man's home to share his hearth the dog was destined to become his faithful friend, ally and support. The training by man of the dog has been described as 'the completest, the most singular and the most useful conquest ever made by man'. The dog soon showed that it was capable of guarding the captured prey, the horse and the reindeer, thus giving man the chance to build up a store of possessions for the first time. So the hand-to-mouth nature of man's existence was modified. At last he was able to lay in stores of flesh, food and furs, secure in the knowledge that these treasures would be safely guarded by his dogs.

Hunting

Once the dog had been taken
into the family of mankind, it
then started to assert the
characteristics for which it is
still so much valued the world
over to this day. It barked as a
warning, thus warding off
enemies. It was the first beast of
burden, carrying game, animal
skins and branches, later being
harnessed to the first primitive
form of sledge.

With its keen sense of smell,
and being infinitely fleeter of
foot than man, it was natural that
the next step was for the dog to
assist with hunting. This must
have proved one of the most
difficult lessons of all, for it had
to be taught to give up the prey
it had caught or retrieved, and
this must have gone against its
deepest instincts. It also had to
be taught to lie obediently for
lengths of time on command,
guarding the captured animals,
an action which, if practised in
the wild, would have been
tantamount to suicide.

The dog then started to show the characteristics for which it is so
much valued to this day. It barked as a warning and to ward off
enemies. It assisted in the hunting with its keen sense of smell and
speed. It became a faithful companion, with its ever adoring look and
its constant attempts to snuggle closer to its master. In some respects
we appear to have reached a turning point in our relationship with the
dog. With increasing urbanisation, the rise of an eloquent lobby
against hunting, the cult of owning large and ferocious animals as a
protection against criminals, and, one must frankly admit, the increase
in irresponsible and unthinking dog owners, there is now a strong tide
of opinion running against dogs. There are calls for licensing,
registration, better control and severe penalties for those who allow
their dogs to become a nuisance. Whether these restrictions and the
use of the law to control dog owners will be effective is something
that can be argued over by the opposing groups who support one or
the other points of view. What is unarguable is that dog owners must
be educated from early childhood to practise good and sensible
ownership. Otherwise, the anti-dog lobby will grow and eventually
sour this country's passion for dogs. It will also destroy the image
described in the following lines by Lord Byron which appear at the
beginning of each Annual Report of The Dogs Home Battersea.

*With eye upraised, his master's looks to scan,
The joy, the solace, and the aid of man;
The rich man's guardian and the poor man's friend,
The only creature faithful to the end.*

J.A. Hare
Director General
The Dogs Home Battersea

Opposite:
Borzois on the look-out

Making the Most of Your Dog

Most of us cannot resist the appealing beauty of a tiny pup tumbling prettily around its mother in the breeder's kennels, or the haunting sadness of a small canine waif in a rescue home. Yet for every person whose heart is touched, there is at least one puppy who will turn its new home into total chaos as soon as it arrives. Within minutes it will have made one mess or another on the floor. Within days it will almost certainly have chewed a treasured possession or piece of furniture to the point of uselessness, reduced a favourite rose tree to a frazzled toothbrush, cut human sleep to a minimum, removed some of the paint from a few doors, and caused terror by apparently swallowing a variety of unsuitable objects. By this time the puppy will be at its most appealing when asleep. When awake it is perhaps best described as an alimentary canal with a formidable means of destruction at one end, and no responsibility at the other.

After such an introduction, you may well wonder why this chapter is entitled 'Making the Most of Your Dog'. No other creature offers so much affection, loyalty, forgiveness and friendship. No other creature has volunteered for domestication, coming willingly to the campfire of man and offering him undivided devotion.

The first dog training session probably took place some 12,000 years or so ago, and communication between man and dog has been developing steadily ever since. The stories of canine devotion to human beings are legion; a devotion reflected in the large number of canine companions on farms, in a wide variety of working situations, out walking in field and park, or just curled up in a favourite armchair. The bond of friendship can be built up to such an extent that a dog will understand what is required even before it is told. Dogs have even been known to mimic with a lopsided grin the smiles and laughter of their masters. They have adapted to domesticity amazingly well and have become used to us. They don't want to change or improve us. They just accept us as we are – wrinkles, faults and all.

The domesticated dog can always be recommended as a fine companion BUT any human being contemplating taking on a dog should know what he or she is in for. In return for the devotion and intelligent companionship of a dog, one must care for it throughout its life and readily accept full responsibility twenty-four hours a day.

Opposite:
Dogs accept us completely – faults and all

16

Opposite:
This Golden Retriever is a picture of the affectionate intelligent companion

Puppies are so appealing – these Welsh Springers being no exception – but they are capable of causing total destruction in minutes!

If your dog knows you care it will grow and thrive as a well-adjusted friend. When we take on this major responsibility with its furry coat, big eyes, waving tail, wet tongue, mobile ears, and unique personality, it becomes very demanding, of affection and care. It will cost money to feed and keep healthy. It will be a 'tie' to the home, with holidays and days out a little more difficult to arrange. It will need almost as much love as a person, regular exercise and grooming. Almost certainly, it will take over your most comfortable chair, your house, your garden – and your heart if you are lucky. Depending on the breed, your dog may need special care: extensive grooming for a long-haired breed; more exercise for a large breed; special training for a heavy, potentially aggressive type. The garden will need to be made escape proof. These are just a few of the many considerations, depending on individual owner-and-dog circumstances.

Making the most of your dog – or perhaps letting him, or her make the most of you – requires a special understanding. When he arrives

DUSKY

Dusky was a black and white Border Collie who had been born on a Cotswold farm. He was collected by his master when barely three months old. Placed in a cardboard box on the back seat of the car he started his journey back to Devonshire. He soon wriggled free, however, and got himself on to the floor, where he curled up and went to sleep, not stirring until he reached his destination, three and a half hours later.

He quickly took to his new life and began to accompany his master everywhere. Sometimes 600 miles a week would be covered by car but with frequent runs in between, he loved it, sitting up beside the driver and taking an interest in everything that passed by. He was only five or six months old when during a business trip to Yorkshire he seized the chance to show how great a part instinct plays in his breed.

It was on a journey over the high road in Wensleydale, Yorkshire, some miles from Hawes, that a stop was made to give him a stretch. There was not a soul or vehicle in sight. Just minutes later he was gone. His boss was frantic and then high up on the top of the moor a movement caught his eye and there was Dusky rounding up a large flock of sheep – quite professional about it he was too. The horn was blown – an understood recall signal – whistles and calls were all to no avail. He was in full cry. His owner started the car and drove along the road keeping pace with the

sheep above, then fortunately one sheep showed initiative and took off down the hillside to the road. Dusky followed and was caught.

Most dogs when they pant appear to laugh and he was no exception – in fact he *did* laugh. If he could have talked he would have said: 'Wow, that was worth all the scolding – what a run!' He soon learnt that rounding up sheep or cattle was not in his curriculum and there was never any more trouble.

He quickly proved a most intelligent, easy-to-train dog and never in his life did he have to be put on a lead. When told to stay close, he did. Having learned the command 'stay' nothing would move him until his master gave the word. Once he was left at the entrance to a big store and his master forgot him, leaving by another door. Three hours later he was still there. Usually it was impossible to forget him for he never let 'the boss' out of his sight. With children he was marvellous and on one occasion at a tea party a whole tray of cream cakes was accidentally dropped on the floor at his feet. Here was a spread which delighted his heart but he did not move – not even a twitch of ear or whisker until the worst of the mess was cleared and he was given the word to dispose of the remnants. All, to the last crumb, disappeared in a twinkling.

An amazing thing was his memory at hotels. On the second stay at any of them he would go straight to the lift and even with several months' interval would invariably go to the room they had last occupied. By his splendid nature he made himself a firm favourite at each and was greeted by the staff with a pleasure not sometimes accorded to humans.

For ten years Dusky was the 'king of the castle' at home and in due course there were two additions to the household in the shape of a dog and a cat.

The years passed and Dusky, who had suffered few ailments in his life began to slow down badly and his trouble was diagnosed as cancer. At his end he lay down to enable the vet to inject for the last time as obediently and sedately as he had all his life.

He was eleven years of age and in the years since never a day passes without someone in the western counties where he was very well known, recalling his beautiful disposition and intelligence.

Naturally a sadness fell over the household and Ben, the dog, and Esther, the cat, just kept looking everywhere for their elder statesman.

Dusky was a black and white Border Collie

THREE FAITHFUL COLLIES

The controversy over the intelligence of animals will perhaps never be resolved. There are those who are certain that animals have only instinct; others are convinced of their capacity for reasoning. Whatever the answer, animals often leave us amazed at their behaviour in difficult or dangerous circumstances.

One such example must surely be that of the three sheepdogs belonging to a shepherd living near Callendar in the Trossachs district of Scotland. The shepherd left the farm, accompanied by his three dogs, at 9am on a winter's morning to see to the 1,200 sheep in his care, some of which were missing beyond the great hills which form a backcloth to the little town. But the weather deteriorated badly and he failed to return. He had been missing eleven hours when the alarm was raised by the arrival back at the farm of one of his collies. The twin hazards of heavy snowfall and thick fog made it impossible to start a search that night, but next morning an RAF mountain-rescue team, police, foresters, shepherds, gamekeepers and a helicopter mounted a search.

The weather was still atrocious and the helicopter had to be withdrawn, but those on foot struggled on. Eventually one of the police constables, making slow progress through the snow and mist, was halted by a deep growl. He found the two collies standing guard over the body of their master. All night they had waited in those awful conditions, and now they were ready to attack the constable as he approached. Soft snow on the hills had yielded beneath the shepherd's weight and he had fallen 500ft to his death. The people of the Trossachs mourned the loss of one whom they had held in great affection and esteem.

One wonders what sort of reasoning went on in the minds of those dogs. Humans in the same situation would have considered which of them could best make the return journey and raise the alarm. Perhaps they would have tossed a coin for it. In the same way, two of the animals elected to stay on guard, while the other went for help.

---

in the lounge wet and muddy from an exhilarating romp with the cat in the compost heap, he will be genuinely surprised when the human he loves so dearly and with whom he wishes to share the joy of his experience, shrieks and yells at him. He believes that the enthusiasm he feels for an encounter with a smelly hedgehog carcase should be shared, and the scolding he receives for rolling in it is difficult for him to understand. If you can forgive him as fast as he can forgive you – usually in about the time it takes for you to tie your shoelace – then you are almost there! Dogs behave strangely, have odd habits, react peculiarly at times. They are, however, dogs, not human beings. As they struggle to understand your many peculiarities, so you need to learn about theirs. For instance, imagine how a dog feels when he wants to be let out and his TV watching master continues to ignore him. Or, if the dog was taking ages to get your dinner, would you not try to attract some attention? If you were overfed or shut up in the house with no access to a loo, perhaps you too would have an accident or two!

So, in order to make the most of your dog, you have to set about understanding him, and you have to help him to understand you. While each dog (and each human) is different, there are some common characteristics. Most dogs are anxious to please, and encouragement and praise go a long way to making a dog responsive and cheerful about doing what is required of him. A firm human response to bad behaviour, showing that you are the boss, is also needed, but it is far from necessary to over-react. Any discipline administered must be in canine, not human, terms. Speak to him so

Sunshine Sherry

It was a grey, cold morning and Sherry, the Miniature Dachshund was curled up in her basket. Presently the day brightened and a little patch of sunlight appeared on the floor. Sherry got up and went to lie in the sun but was fidgetty. I watched, fascinated, as she went back to the basket and, with much effort, overturned it. Seizing the cushion firmly, she dragged it across the room into the patch of sun. After two or three turns to make it comfortable, she settled down with a little sigh of satisfaction and promptly went to sleep.

Canine thought processes in action? This seems to come close to reasoning power.

Faithful friends

It is possible that man originally hunted dogs for food, and then, having cornered and captured a bitch either in whelp or already with her pups, decided to rear them as stock. It is easy to imagine him succumbing to the evident charms of those puppies, and from the closer relationship that would then have developed he might have begun to realise the potential of this new relationship. Once taken into man's home to share his hearth, the dog was destined to become his faithful friend, ally and support.

If you do not want your dog on the sofa, make sure he knows it from the beginning – and be consistent

that he understands you. He is frequently bewildered by the strange antics of the human: the inconsistency of command, the sudden explosion of temper, the days when nothing seems to go right. A dog will not understand, for example, if he is always allowed on the best settee except when he has been rolling in horse manure, or searching for fish in the depths of the river. You have to ensure that he stays off by keeping him away from the best settee until he is clean and dry – not as a punishment, either, but as part of his care routine.

Spend as much time as you can with a dog. The more you are with him the better you get to know, appreciate and learn about each other. It will not be long before you are able to rely on him – but make sure that he can then rely on *you* too. Talk to your dog as much as you can; never mind the curious glances from passers-by. Your dog will appreciate it and learn about your voice, your words, your means of communication. Observe your dog, at play, when eating, when searching, even when asleep, and you will understand him better. Be assured he will be watching you, too, just to find out how you behave.

Praise your dog whenever there is an opportunity to do so. There is no need to stuff him full of gastronomic rewards. A kind word or two and some fussing is quite enough and of much more value. If you have to scold him, forgive him as soon as you can. It is quite useless extending the reprimand after he has forgotten about it; and you

Taking over the most comfortable chair

cannot remind him about it later, because he just will not understand. It is frequently said that slapping the rump of a puppy with a rolled-up newspaper is the best way of teaching it not to mess on the carpet. Fine, but do you always carry a rolled-up newspaper around with you? While you are searching for one and rolling it up, the puppy will have forgotten the incident. Something akin to bewilderment then follows when the human he was just beginning to understand descends on him and clouts him with a noisy newspaper roll. His short memory helps him to forgive you too, if you tread on his paw or trip over him!

Be consistent with feeding times, exercise etc. Dogs enjoy routine and should be able to rely on regular attention to their needs. Do not keep changing his diet, which will probably upset his stomach.

Consider your dog's needs as you would any other member of the family. If taking him on a long car journey, is there food and water for him, does he have enough room, will he be too hot, is he car-sick? Has he been thoroughly dried after a wet walk? Is he outgrowing his bed? Is he being groomed regularly enough? Does he appear a little off-colour today? Is he being given enough attention to prevent boredom? Has his drinking-water dish been washed and refilled today? Remember that your dog has to rely *entirely* on you for his needs. He is totally in your hands.

Above all, go out of your way to make your dog happy. Today's descendants of those Ice Age canine toughies have pretty well got their act together. They *want* to please; they *want* to be loved. Although, like any other living creature, they too have their moments of mischief, they will *try* to be good companions. If as much could be said for all dog owners, the world would be a great place for dogs – and, incidentally, not such a bad one for humans either.

CLEOPATRA, PHONE FANATIC

Of course, it all depends on the outlook! Some people have a telephone installed because it is a necessity, a vital link with the outside world. To others it is just a convenience, and there are those who feel bound to have it but regard it as a curse, a noisy nuisance or an interfering menace (author is in this last category).

At a house in Old Windsor, Berkshire, another attitude prevails. The strident burr is treated as a direct assault on the occupants of the house, from which they must be protected at all costs. So, every time the telephone rings there is a mad dash to hook the receiver off its rest. No wonder callers are somewhat disconcerted to hear growls and barks, and sometimes they are cut off altogether.

This is Cleopatra in action! Cleo is an eight-year-old Jack Russell terrier and has been a phone fanatic from puppyhood. Whenever the phone rings she dashes to it, lifts the receiver and carries if off to her basket nearby. Unless Mrs Nash her owner gets there first – and she is rarely quick enough – she is lucky if she can rescue the receiver in time to take the call.

All the family friends have complained of the cavalier treatment they receive on the phone, but when the boss wants to call Mr Nash urgently and cannot get through, it is no longer a laughing matter. So recently, after redecorating, the Nashes decided that perhaps a better place for the phone was on the wall, nicely out of Cleo's reach. The first few calls after that meant wild jumps to get at it, but Cleo is quick to learn; within twenty-four hours she realised there was a better way and she raced up the stairs to get at the second instrument in the bedroom. That is what she still does, though the humans now have a sporting chance of answering the phone first.

Cleo came to the Nash household when she was nine weeks old and is as bright as can be on many things. When the British Broadcasting Company heard about her antics, she was invited to appear on the television network. She behaved beautifully and showed to the cameras none of the antagonism that she has to the phone. She is a television enthusiast herself and will watch intently with scarcely a movement for an hour or more at a time. Football is her favourite viewing. When, however, the advertisements for dog foods appear, she hurls herself at the screen, whether for the food or at the dogs which usually take part no one can decide.

Cleo had a bad bout of illness recently and part of the treatment was the rationing of her drinking water to very small amounts at two-hourly intervals only. After the first day of pleading – and it was quite a heart-breaking experience for her mistress – Cleo worked out a possible solution. She simply went to the bathroom and sat under the shower, just hoping that someone would come in and turn it on.

The great Cleopatra of history captivated many by her charms. Cleopatra of Old Windsor also captivates people by her charms when they meet her, but not – certainly not – when she answers the telephone!

Cleopatra has been a phone fanatic since puppyhood

Guard duties

Baron Cuvier (1769-1832), the great French anatomist and naturalist, described the training by man of the dog as 'the completest, the most singular and the most useful conquest ever made by man'. It is beyond dispute that the ownership of property is one of the bases upon which civilisation has been developed, and the dog soon showed that it was capable of guarding the captured prey, the horse and the reindeer, thus making it possible for man to build up a store of possessions for the first time. So the hand-to mouth nature of man's existence was modified. At last he was able to lay in stores of flesh, food and furs, secure in the knowledge that the guardianship of these treasures would be safely taken care of by his dogs.

CAN A DOG SYMPATHISE?

That animals, particularly dogs, have feeling and understanding is obvious to people who either own or study them. Even so, dog lovers are occasionally astounded by the degree of sensitivity shown by their pets, sometimes in the most unlikely circumstances. How often, for instance, does a dog in a car make apparent his like or dislike of another on the pavement, even when the car is travelling quite fast and one would have thought that there was no time for reactions!

Hamish was a dour Scotch Terrier owned by Mr and Mrs R.F. Hartill of Nuneaton in Warwickshire. So jealously did he guard the premises that he would not allow either cat or dog to put a nose in the front gate. He would sit at the window for long periods, swaying slightly to and fro – and if a trespasser dared to invade he would go berserk, tearing out of the house with rugs and mats flying and skidding in his wake. They were rare and brave spirits who managed to stand their ground before such an onslaught.

The family were all the more surprised one day when Hamish was seen to be escorting a woebegone little mongrel up the drive and gently nosing him down to the doormat by the front door. It was all the more amazing because this was his own special holy of holies. Having settled the stranger on to the mat, he then went to recruit human help. This visitor was obviously a stray – dirty, cold, hungry and very, very scared. They took him in and bathed him, Hamish watching approvingly and adding an occasional lick of his own. The stray was then fed from Hamish's bowl and put for the night in Hamish's bed without the slightest protest from him. In due course the dog's owner was found, but Hamish was the courteous host right to the end.

How much perception and understanding? We shall never know, but it was all so out of character that only some deeply embedded instinct could have given rise to such impeccable behaviour.

A Day in the Life of The Dogs Home Battersea

Just over the Chelsea Bridge, between the old Battersea Power Station and the Gas Works, a tuneless choir rises as buckets clank and gates swing to. Six hundred and one hopeful faces look down the line.

It is not a scene from *Oliver Twist* but a typical day at England's – and possibly the world's – largest sanctuary for lost and abandoned dogs. In an average year, the kennels and yards shelter more than 22,000 dogs and 850 cats.

Latest arrival on parade

*This must be Battersea –
one of the red ambulances arrives
with its daily cargo of lost and
abandoned dogs*

Since The Dogs Home Battersea first opened its doors in 1860, nearly 2¾ million dogs have been given refuge. And last year alone, the Home received more than 86,000 human visitors.

Battersea today is a very far cry from its beginnings in Hollingsworth Street, Islington, North London. Removed to its present site in 1871, the Home was enlarged in 1907, and the older portion was largely rebuilt. Incorporated in 1933, it became a registered charity in 1960. In 1975, a large rebuilding project for new kennels, a cattery and a veterinary clinic was completed. Further extensions have been made over the years but the most important new feature is the modern veterinary clinic which opened in 1985. Plans are also well advanced for the complete refurbishment of the famous arches and the building of a new three-storey kennel block for two hundred dogs on the present ambulance garage site.

The Home is open for the acceptance of dogs twenty-four hours a day, seven days a week, all the year round, even Christmas Day. The public, as well as prospective buyers, are welcome to look round the

Home for a small charge. The chief objectives are to restore lost dogs to their owners; to give food and temporary shelter; to provide good homes for dogs at reasonable prices and to provide an instantaneous and painless death for those that have to be destroyed.

In an ideal situation, everyone would buy their pets from the Home. This would stop unscrupulous breeders who take advantage of people's ignorance in the sale of supposedly pedigree dogs. But it has also been found from long experience that Battersea dogs, whose experience of people has usually been one of cruelty leading to fear and distrust, become passionately devoted to those who show them kindness and loving care.

Tucked beneath the arches of the old Victoria to Dover Railway, along which still thunders many a coastal bound train, The Dogs Home is the centre to which every stray dog in the London Metropolitan Police area is delivered. The system in London is similar to that operating throughout Britain; stray dogs are taken to the nearest police station where they are kept overnight, then collected by one of the Home's ambulances the next day.

Promptly at six o'clock every morning, a teleprinter message is sent from Scotland Yard, London's police headquarters, to The Dogs Home, listing all police stations within its very large area which have dogs for collection. The task of collection is carried out by the five-van fleet of scarlet animal ambulances whose drivers report for duty well before the Home opens to the public for business. Armed with a rota, they make their way to an allotted number of police stations returning around lunch time to off-load the dogs.

Emergency conditions

This is a list of conditions that demand immediate veterinary treatment. They are listed in random order. Other conditions may need urgent treatment too, but this list does indicate the kind of emergency that could occur with a dog.

Cardiac failure
Bone fractures
Severe respiratory difficulties
Whelping complications
Massive haemorrhage
Prolonged diarrhoea
Severe wounds
Convulsions
Shock
Urine retention
Heatstroke
Evident pain
Penetrating wounds of chest
    or abdomen
Extensive burns or scalds
Hernia strangulation
Coma or loss of
    consciousness
Swallowed foreign body
Spinal fractures
Grass seed in ear etc
Skull damage
Kennel cross-infections
Poisoning
Intussusception

A policeman's lot . . .
Sir Peter Imbert QC
Commissioner, Metropolitan
Police during a visit to Battersea

First-aid

Keep a first-aid box stocked for the dog at all times in the home (and perhaps a basic one in the car). Suggested general contents are listed below.

First-aid box contents
Dressings (gauze, sterile)
Vaseline (tube)
Round-tipped scissors
Acriflavine
Round-ended forceps
TCP
Clinical thermometer
Eucalyptus oil
Medicine dropper and
      rubber teats
Worming tablets
Veterinary deodorant
Plastic syringes (20ml)
Alugan sachets
     (flea shampoo
     treatment)
Stainless steel dish
Clean towelling
Bandages
Disprin
Absorbent lint
Epsom salts
Cottonwool balls
Sodium bicarbonate
Double-sided surgical tape

The waifs and strays are mostly found by the police, many of them in a state of severe neglect. Practically every breed comes to the Home, from St Bernards and Afghans to Chihuahuas and Pekinese. It is strange how anybody could lose anything as big as a Saint Bernard, but people do! Of course many of them are genuinely lost and are claimed very quickly, but a large number do not get claimed at all.

On arrival at the Home, the dogs are carefully examined by the veterinary staff, given a vaccination against all the dog diseases, a numbered collar disc and a meal. The numbers are then entered on the central register, so that if there is a controversy over ownership a check can be made to establish the area from which the dog came. Members of the public who call to look for a missing dog are required to fill in a comprehensive questionnaire stating where the dog was lost, and when, giving its age, sex and other details. There have been instances in which people have attempted to claim a dog that did not belong to them, but this detailed information allows the staff to decide if a claimant is telling the truth when he/she says 'Ah, yes, that is my dog'.

Under the law, a dog must be kept for seven days pending claim. During this statutory period the Home is maintaining the dogs for the police. It is the police who supply the fee for the period the unclaimed dog is under care.

I'm not going any further until somebody explains!

When the dogs have completed their veterinary inspection and inoculation, they are put into waiting kennels – there are Monday kennels, Tuesday kennels, Wednesday kennels and so on. At the end of the seventh day, the dogs that remain unclaimed are moved over to the sale blocks. The myth that dogs are put down if unclaimed after the seven-day period is totally untrue. Only dogs suffering chronic or debilitating illnesses and very old dogs are humanely destroyed. The number of dogs coming in is about 40-60 per normal day, increasing to 80-90 per day after a bank holiday, and averaging out at about 250 per week. Only about thirteen per cent are reclaimed. However, this is not such a sad reflection on owners, as fifty per cent of all owners rush to their nearest police station the minute they realise their dog is lost, so only half the number of all stray dogs actually find their way into the Home.

The kennels incorporate under-floor heating, infra-red lamps and

*Safely identified by reception,
so where do we go from here?*

Caring hands give the once over . .

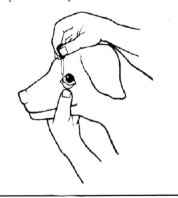

Eye drops

An eye-dropper is a handy object to have around. Dust or grit can often be gently washed from the eye by dropping in slightly warm sterile water (boiled and cooled water can be used). Antibiotic eye-drops are also a convenient means of fighting ophthalmic infection if prescribed by a veterinarian.

Is this the way to my room?

31

EVERY DOG SHOULD OWN A MAN

Every dog should have a man of his own. There is nothing like a well-behaved person around the house to spread the dog's blanket for him, or bring him his supper when he comes home man-tired at night.

For example, I happen to belong to an English setter who acquired me when he was about six months old and has been training me quite successfully ever since. He has taught me to shake hands with him and fetch his ball. I've learned not to tug at the leash when he takes me for a walk. I am completely house broken, and I make him a devoted companion.

The first problem a dog faces is to pick out the right man – a gay and affectionate disposition is more important than an expensive pedigree. I do not happen to be registered but my setter is just as fond of me as though I came from a long line of blue bloods. Also, since a dog is judged by the man he leads, it is a good idea to walk the man up and down a couple of times to make sure his action is free and he has springy hindquarters.

The next question is whether the dog and man should share the house together. Some dogs prefer a kennel because it is more sanitary, but my setter decided at the start that he'd move right in the house with me. I can get into any of the chairs I want except the big overstuffed chair in the living room, which is his.

Training a man takes time. Some men are a little slow to respond, but a dog who makes allowances and tries to put himself in the man's place will be rewarded with a loyal pal. Men are apt to be high-strung and sensitive, and a dog who loses his temper will only break the man's spirit.

Punishment should be meted out sparingly – more can be accomplished by a reproachful look than by flying off the handle. My setter has never raised a paw to me, but he has cured me almost entirely of the habit of running away. When he sees me start to pack my suitcase he just lies down on the floor with his chin on his forepaws and gazes at me sadly. Usually I wind up by cancelling my train reservations.

The first thing to teach a man is to stay at heel. For this lesson the dog should hook one end of a leash to his collar and loop the other end around the man's wrist so he cannot get away. Start down the street slowly, pausing at each telephone pole until the man realises that he's under control. He may tug and yank at first, but this can be discouraged by slipping deftly between his legs and winding the leash around his ankles. If the man tries to run ahead, brace all four feet and halt suddenly, thus jerking him flat on his back. After a few such experiences the man will follow his dog with docility. Remember, however, that all such efforts at discipline must be treated as sport, and after a man has sprawled on the sidewalk the dog should lick his face to show him it was all in fun.

Every man should learn to retrieve a rubber ball. The way my setter taught me this trick was simple. He would lie in the centre of the floor while I carried the ball to the far side of the room and rolled it toward him, uttering the word 'Fetch!' He would watch the ball carefully as it rolled past him and under the sofa. I would then get the ball from under the sofa and roll it past him again, giving the same command, 'Fetch!'

This lesson would be repeated until the setter was asleep. After I got so I would retrieve the ball every time I said 'Fetch!' my dog substituted other articles for me to pick up, such as an old marrow bone or a piece of paper he found in the wastebasket.

The matter of physical conditioning is important. A man whose carriage is faulty, and who slouches and droops his tail, is a reflection on the dog who owns him. The best way to keep him in shape is to work him constantly and never give him a chance to relax. Racing him up and down the street at the end of a leash is a great conditioner. If he attempts to slump into an easy chair when he gets back, the dog should leap into it ahead of him and force him to sit in a straight-backed chair to improve his posture. And be sure to get him up several times a night to go out for a walk, especially if it is raining.

Equally important is diet. Certain liquids such as beer have a tendency to bloat a man, and a dog should teach him restraint by jumping up at him and spilling his drink, or tactfully knocking the glass off the table with a sweep of his tail.

Not every dog who tries to bring up a man is as successful as my setter. The answer lies in understanding. The dog must be patient and not work himself into a tantrum if his man can't learn to chase rabbits or wriggle under fences as well as the dog does. After all, as my setter says, it's hard to teach an old man new tricks.

specially designed fibre-glass dog beds which fit neatly into the width of each kennel. Along with the satellite kennels at Bell Mead, Old Windsor, where long-stay prisoners and hospital dogs are also kept, there are no better kennels to be found anywhere in the country.

Under the arches, nobody 'dreams their dream away', apart from many of the animals. The Home provides a twenty-four hour service. The rounds begin at 7am when the first of the day staff arrives and by 8am the total complement of over thirty will be on duty.

The first task is to clean out. The 463 kennels are cleaned out three to four times a day by a devoted kennel staff. Usually all the kennels are occupied, several by more than one inhabitant. The Home rarely has fewer than 550 – 600 dogs in residence, so often it is the case of doubling or even trebling up. Each kennel must look spanking fresh and smell hygienic when the staff have finished their round. Every cat must have its day too. In the equally well appointed cattery, around eighty cages have to be cleaned thoroughly.

Next, feeds must be prepared. Fully grown, healthy dogs are fed with a well known brand of 'complete' dog food, accompanied of course by plenty of water. This is the main diet, but some tinned food and biscuits may be used too. For ailing animals, and for motherless puppies and kittens, special diets have to be prepared, and in the

The Battersea stamps of 1985 commemorated 125 years, and over 2.5 million stray dogs received

'I failed to keep up with my mortgage repayments'

Sleep

As essential for dogs as it is for all creatures. For puppies it is especially important and they need much more sleep than the adult dog. The need for sleep is still little understood but dogs do sleep a good deal during which tissues rest and are repaired. They are light sleepers and can be disturbed by noise or activities in unfamiliar surroundings.

In sleep, respiration and heart-rate are slower and body temperature falls. There are periods of rapid eye movements (known as REM) during which time the dog may also twitch its limbs and sometimes make little whimpering noises.

Deprivation of sleep can cause ill-health and also alter a dog's personality. Puppies need to be allowed to sleep peacefully whenever they wish to do so, in a warm, comfortable resting place which provides security.

The dog prepares for sleep by seeking out a special place, circling round and round its bed before settling down in a particular sleeping posture, often curled with its head down to its tail. The circling and curling up behaviour may perhaps be a legacy from the wild days of the dog when sleeping outside entailed finding a sheltered spot and turning round and round to make a circular hollow in which to curl up to retain body heat.

A sick dog is helped in many cases by peaceful sleep, allowing healing to take place and tissues to be repaired undisturbed by other body activities. Anxiety, which uses up much energy, is also reduced while the patient is asleep.

kitchens large cauldrons have to be set simmering. Steamed fish and rice, easily digestible, are on the menu for the very sick animal, just as they might be for a poorly human. Other tempting items range from chicken to rabbit.

After the dogs have had breakfast, it is time for them to exercise in the exercise runs. The excitement is high as the inmates are let out of their kennels to play together and run about, and often the noise of their barking can be heard above the roar of the trains overhead.

Though the yards themselves, and adjacent bridge and a faded rooftop sign whisper of bygone days, the Home itself occupies an antiseptic-clean, white-tiled building far different from the Victorian dungeon image. The reception area, with its modern console desk and uniformed staff, feels like a cross between a police station and a veterinarian's waiting room. It serves as a little of both.

By 10.30am, opening time, a small knot of people has gathered outside, although it is not unusual to see a queue waiting at 9.30am; and it has been known for people to spend the night outside. Like clockwork, the doors are opened on time and, on average, 200 – 250 people visit the Home daily, either looking for a lost pet, looking for a new one – or just looking. Bereft owners scribble out answers to a brief questionnaire, then disappear with keepers to scan the kennels for one familiar face.

Prospective owners are carefully screened for suitability and are handed a leaflet which seeks to establish a number of basic facts. Can they afford the upkeep of a dog? Do they wish to breed from the dog? Is their accommodation suitable? Is there an open space nearby where the dog can be exercised? Can they make arrangements for the dog to be looked after when they go on holiday? Is there someone at home during the day to look after the dog? Do they object to a home visit?

The Home warns that it cannot give a guarantee of perfect health or temperament. But, with great fairness, it gives a guarantee that buyers can get their money back. All purchasers have to sign a declaration that the animal will not be used for vivisection or other experimental purposes. Last, but not least, the staff are instructed not to sell a dog if they do not like the look of a customer. And recently, the Home has introduced a system of home visits to try to prevent dogs falling into the wrong hands. Eight Home Visitors are now employed to make random checks at buyers' homes.

Every dog purchased is given a medical check before it is allowed to leave. The purchaser is present throughout the examination and it is here that advice is given on the dog's health, feeding arrangements and the need to take the dog to a vet after seven days.

The Clinic provides an invaluable service to both in-patients and out-patients on Tuesday and Thursday afternoons. The emphasis is on medical work which includes the treatment of skin and other diseases, the mending of broken bones and spaying and neutering. The Clinic treats up to sixty dogs a day in its modern examination rooms and operating theatre.

Rich or poor, customers buying a new pet pay the same price: £25-

Not my usual surroundings you understand

A little encouragement works wonders

Opposite:
*Sam's new home is with
the Chairman*

£55 for a dog, according to breed; around £9.00 for a cat (1989 prices). The reclaim fee charged to owners is only £2.60 plus £4.00 vaccination fee. These prices are kept deliberately low, so it is remarkable that about one-third of Battersea's annual income comes directly from reclaim fees and sales. Another third comes from donations and subscriptions and the remaining third includes receipts from a contract with the Metropolitan Police who are obliged by law to pay for the first seven days' lodging of each dog they send in

About forty-one per cent of the annual intake of dogs which are given food and shelter are found new homes. However, there is still a disturbing pattern of gross neglect by dog-owners. The pattern has not changed much in recent years. Puppies and kittens are still rescued from dustbins and rubbish tips, dogs are still found roaming the streets, or running pathetically beside a motorway or railway line. Just after Christmas there is the usual significant increase in pets bought as presents for children and turned out once the family has got tired of the new 'toy'. And every summer there is a surge in the intake caused by heartless people going on holiday and abandoning their pets. There is also a steady daily trickle of people bringing in their

---

Good taste

Mongrels who are discriminating about their food tend to live to a great age. Rory Patterson, for example, clocked up nineteen healthy years on an almost entirely vegetarian diet. He hated meat and wouldn't touch bones, preferring grapefruit, cheese and chocolate. Sinbad Rowlands loved chocolate and reached twenty-one years by having a bar to himself every night. Peter Ferris actually suffered from digestive trouble when he was eighteen months. The vet forbade him to eat dog biscuits or tinned food, prescribing just brown bread and baked breast of lamb. On this simple diet, livened up by an occasional sweet biscuit, Peter, a handsome gold and white Prop Forward, lasted a record twenty-one-and-a-half years, and kept his elegant figure to the day he died.

*Could I take them all please –
it's so difficult to make a choice*

Please choose me, we're made for each other

Boredom

A dog can be affected mentally and physically by boredom and reasons for it should be carefully avoided. A dog (and especially a puppy) which lacks companionship, perhaps being left alone in the house all day, will inevitably become bored. As a result it will become mischievous (in order to amuse itself), aggressive (through frustration) or withdrawn and eventually physically ill. The more intelligent the dog, the more easily it can become bored without company, regular exercise and its owner's sustained interest in it.

Below:
Clinching the deal

pets because they can no longer care for them. The imploring looks of the dogs defy resistance but fundamentally, layman and expert agree. The message is 'take care of your dogs and give them a chance'.

The afternoon wears on and gradually the kennel staff goes home. But The Dogs Home Battersea never closes. Someone is on duty every night, to make the rounds, answer the telephone or calls at the gate; until the next day dawns, the fleet of red ambulances fan out across London and the rounds begin again at 7 o'clock.

Step out smartly there – I'm on my way home!

Bootsie

As mongrels are happiest when they are shadowing their owners, it is a great hardship for them to be left in charge of possessions. The Dogs Home Battersea tells a heartbreaking story about a little grey and white Vertical Shagpile who was found guarding an old pair of shoes on a Charing Cross platform during the rush hour. He had obviously been dumped by his master, who'd left him in charge of the shoes, but no one could get near him. In the end a policeman had to catch him with a noose on the end of a pole, and arrived at Battersea holding the dog on a lead with one hand, and the old pair of shoes in the other. Freddie Reed, one of the great *Daily Mirror* photographers, came down to the Home and took pictures of the dog still clinging to his shoes, and reached the pinnacle of his fame when the editor cleared the middle page. English hearts were, as usual, touched, and 700 people wrote in offering Bootsie (as he was now called) a home. In the end he went to live with a hairdresser in Bristol, whose home was over the shop, so Bootsie would never be left alone again. He settled in very happily, was gradually weaned from his shoes and Battersea receives a Christmas card every year from Bootsie and his new mistress.

LIST OF BREEDS RECEIVED IN 1988 BY THE DOGS HOME BATTERSEA

	RECEIVED	SOLD	CLAIMED
German Shepherd Dog	1,614	582	225
Jack Russell	742	382	135
Dobermann	685	291	106
Staffordshire Bull Terrier	343	60	115
Labrador Retriever	306	129	108
Collies (all types)	278	121	73
Spaniels (all types)	189	98	36
Rottweiler	173	46	48
Yorkshire Terrier	171	70	59
Greyhound	157	63	27
Lurcher	152	62	17
Boxer	111	52	26
Bull Terrier	67	6	19
Poodle	62	32	16
Retriever	58	27	24
Old English Sheep Dog	52	24	16
King Charles Spaniel	46	25	21
Cairn Terrier	44	20	20
West Highland White Terrier	41	16	13
Irish Setter	38	13	15
Whippet	30	11	10
Shih Tzu	26	10	11
Great Dane	26	10	4
Weimaraner	16	9	4
Chihuahua	16	7	4
Dalmatian	16	8	6
Shetland Sheepdog	15	10	3
Dachshund	14	7	3
Pointer	13	9	3
Afghan Hound	12	4	4
Basset Hound	12	9	3
Pomeranian	12	6	3
Airedale	11	5	5
Corgi	10	3	5
Samoyed	10	5	5

	RECEIVED	SOLD	CLAIMED
Schnauzer	10	6	4
Beagle	9	7	1
Lhasa Apso	9	8	Nil
Pekingese	8	3	2
Rhodesian Ridgeback	8	5	1
Fox Terrier	7	3	3
Mastiff	7	3	3
St Bernard	7	3	2
Chow Chow	6	1	3
Bulldog	6	4	Nil
Border Terrier	4	1	Nil
Groenendael	4	3	1
Scottish Terrier	4	1	1
Lakeland Terrier	3	2	Nil
Wolfhound	3	1	1
Bichon Frise	2	1	1
Basenji	2	2	Nil
Chinese Crested	2	1	1
English Setter	2	Nil	2
Kerry Blue Terrier	2	Nil	1
Miniature Pinscher	2	Nil	2
Siberian Husky	2	Nil	2
Saluki	2	Nil	1
Tibetan Terrier	2	2	Nil
Sydney Silky	2	2	Nil
Bedlington Terrier	1	Nil	Nil
Akita	1	1	Nil
Anatolian Karabash	1	Nil	1
Borzois	1	Nil	1
Briard	1	1	Nil
Gordon Setter	1	Nil	1
Keeshond	1	Nil	1
Bloodhound	1	Nil	Nil
Alaskan Malamute	1	1	Nil
Munsterlander	1	Nil	1
Manchester Terrier	1	1	Nil
Norwegian Buhund	1	Nil	1
Otterhound	1	Nil	1
Pug	1	1	Nil
Shipperke	1	Nil	1
Welsh Terrier	1	Nil	Nil
Mongrels	15,099	6,709	1,722
TOTAL	**21,004**		

Homing instinct

Michael Fox, in his book *Understanding your Dog,* suggests that some dogs may have a homing instinct, like carrier pigeons, and are able to navigate by the angle of the sun or the stars. If a dog is separated from home (or the place he considers he ought to be) his internal clock tells him there is an incongruity between the time of day he feels inside him, and the time of day the sun is registering by virtue of its position. He then sets out in the direction that will reduce this internal and external difference. Once he gets near home, he will pick up familiar smells and sights and find his way more easily.

and sixth sense

How do dogs trace owners to places where the dog has never been? There was for example a mongrel in the First World War who, never having been out of England before, crossed the channel and found his master in the trenches. Then there was the mongrel called Tony, who was left in the care of friends because his owners had moved from Illinois to a town in Michigan some 225 miles away. Somehow, six weeks later, Tony, wearing his identifying collar and disc, turned up at the Michigan home. Such feats must defy the rational mind and it is here we enter the tricky world of ESP or 'Psi-trailing', as it is called, which means the psychic location of where someone is. Perhaps in the same way that the mongrel in Australia 'knew' his mistress had landed, Tony and the dog in the First World War were drawn by some sixth sense to their owners. T. S. Eliot wrote of lovers 'who think the same thoughts without need of speech.' Perhaps dogs, whose devotion exceeds that of most lovers, are able to pick up telepathic vibrations from beloved owners who are constantly thinking and worrying about them.

The New Dog or Puppy

Difficult dogs

Certain breeds and some individual dogs are harder to discipline, especially if they have a lot of natural energy. If you think that your dog falls into this category and you encounter difficulty in training him, you should seek expert advice. Your vet should be able to tell you about local dog training clubs.

Cocker Spaniel, Yorkshire Terrier, Pembroke Corgi – which would you choose?

There is much which is commonsense in choosing a puppy or adult dog. Once you have accepted that you will be totally responsible for its life, welfare, health, and happiness, it is a case of which you most like and to which your lifestyle is best suited.

Let us for the moment assume that you have decided on a puppy – with all that it means in terms of training and understanding. Which puppy do you choose? All puppies are lovable. Like most baby creatures they all have great appeal, but you must take into consideration what it will grow into! Never, for example, buy a puppy only because it is well displayed in a pet-shop window. First decide what the adult dog will eventually be like. Is it a boisterous or quiet breed? Will it grow into a large, small or medium-sized adult? Will it need more than average exercise, or less? Will its coat be long

or short? How big will its appetite be? Will it need special training or control?

All these questions need to be answered before a puppy is purchased. You should not buy a very large breed if you live fifteen floors up in an apartment building, nor should you choose a breed that will require a good deal of exercise if you live in an urban area miles from open spaces and have no car. These may seem obvious points, but many would-be puppy owners neglect them – at a sad cost to the dog.

Do make sure that you have fully considered the implications of owning a puppy and that you have settled on the most suitable breed (or mongrel) for your lifestyle and home facilities. There are around 350 different breeds of dog available and a number of fine cross-bred animals which can be obtained from rescue homes or from unwanted litters. The choice among mongrels is almost unlimited. The choice

Even Rottweilers were young once. Think carefully about the needs of the adult dog before purchasing a puppy – for the dog's sake, as well as your own

Don't take the children

Please do not take children with you when you go to choose a puppy. They may well want a different puppy from the one you choose, and they are bound to be upset if you decide not to have any of the litter. Puppies need to be in a calm environment, and the last thing they need is to be with upset children. And while we are on the subject of children, please do not take them to matings, either, because they are normally not allowed, however well-behaved they may be.

Dog or bitch?

Companionship and faithfulness are not a question of sex – any more than in human life but people do have preferences! A bitch will come into season, resulting in a spotting of blood for several days about twice a year. This really need be no problem but some people are more fussy than others. A male dog, on the other hand, may become something of a nuisance when local bitches come into season. Of course, a bitch can be spayed and a dog neutered if you are not intending to breed.

Some people claim that bitches are cleaner and/or easier to train, but other owners maintain there is no difference! It all boils down to different dog personalities and owner preferences.

between pedigree or mongrel depends entirely on the preference of the potential owner. All dogs are individuals, each with its own character and personality, and there is a wide variety of character types and temperaments. Terriers and spaniels, for example, are very different breed families but each has its own devoted following. Appeal, as well as beauty, is in the eye of the beholder.

There are many good books available (from libraries and bookshops) on individual breeds, and some on the whole range of breeds. The latter books may be of value if you have absolutely no idea which dog to choose.

You need to be clear about the main purpose of buying a dog: for showing, breeding, working, or primarily as a companion. A Pekinese will rarely be helpful in rounding up your ducks at the end of the day, while a Border Collie or Welsh Springer Spaniel can usually be relied upon to respond to appropriate training. A German Shepherd, while needing much more training and control than a Dachshund, will generally be a more effective guard of your property, but the latter will require considerably less exercise, less food and less space.

If a show dog is needed, you will have to pay more and you will need to select a dog from a reputable breeder who conforms to breed standards laid down by the Kennel Club. A similar situation arises if you plan to breed from your dog. A show dog may also turn out not to be ideal if you are looking for an affectionate pet.

A pedigree puppy should be purchased from a reputable breeder, though some adult pedigree dogs can also be found at rescue homes. The local branch of the appropriate breed club will put you in touch with a reputable breeder. (The Kennel Club will provide a list of breed association addresses.)

If you finally decide on a mongrel as your canine companion, the choice is wide indeed. The Dogs Home Battersea, The National Canine Defence League, the RSPCA and local rescue organisations and dogs' homes in most areas will welcome enquiries. Your local veterinarian may also know of a source of healthy animals. While sometimes it may be difficult to predict the eventual size of a mongrel when it is fully grown, your veterinarian can usually give you a general idea of how large a puppy will grow. Local advertisements are another way of finding a puppy or adult dog. Wherever possible, try to see the parents of a puppy, as this will provide you with an idea not only of eventual size, but of temperament and character too.

There can be many advantages to obtaining an adult dog rather than a puppy. In some circumstances, a puppy may not be desirable due to lack of available time for training, and elderly people often prefer the less rigorous demands and less boisterous behaviour of a new adult dog. Whatever the reason, there are many lovable adult dogs in need of homes and available from the sources mentioned above. If you do hear of an adult dog, try to make the dog's acquaintance before accepting him. See if he 'likes' you, and vice versa. Try to discover some of the dog's background, if possible, and be ready to make allowances for his adjustment to an entirely new home and surroundings.

Do not buy either puppy or adult dog from street traders or markets, where animals are often unhealthy: nor from pet shops that are obviously badly equipped, inadequate, or unable to provide full background information on the dogs for sale. Some pet shops are well run, of course, but a visit will soon confirm this. Even commercial breeders can be ill-equipped, resulting in unhealthy puppies. If you discover such circumstances, do inform the RSPCA so that a check can be made on the establishment.

When choosing a puppy, spend some time with the litter if possible, and look for a perky, healthy character with a cheerful disposition. It should move well, with straight limbs and a confident

What's in a name? Non-pedigrees can be beautiful too, and the alert and friendly expressions on these dogs faces more than make up for their lack of ancestry

A safe and comfortable place to sleep will help the new arrival feel at home

Opposite:
An extrovert black Labrador pup enjoys a game with his owner, safely enclosed in the back garden

approach without being too boisterous. Its teeth should be set well, with the upper rows resting over and on those below. The body should be free of any rash and the coat smooth and shiny. The navel should be free of protrusions which indicate a hernia (though this can be corrected by a veterinarian).

PROS & CONS OF DOG V BITCH?

Check it over to make sure there are no evident abnormalities and arrange a veterinary examination as soon as possible after taking it home. The choice between dog or bitch again depends on personal preference.

The puppy you choose from a breeder should have already been wormed. You will need to treat it again later, around three months of age. Ask the breeder for a diet sheet, preferably before collecting the puppy, so that you are aware of what your new puppy has been eating. It is advisable not to make any sudden changes in diet at this stage. The new environment, strange faces, smells, and noises will be enough for it to tackle without a sudden dietary change which will be likely to upset its stomach.

Normally, you will see a puppy at the breeder's home a while before it is ready to leave the litter, so you will have time to make

*Here's one in the eye for you!
This lively trio of Chihuahua pups
are obviously in fine fettle*

The pedigree puppy

It is important that a pedigree puppy should be registered at the Kennel Club. The Club is currently in the process of changing its system of registration. This means that if you buy a pedigree puppy and there is any likelihood of your showing, working or breeding from it, you would be well advised to ensure that it is already registered (ie has a name, number and its parents included on the 'birth certificate'). If you acquire an unregistered dog over twelve months of age, you will find it virtually impossible and certainly expensive to register. So buy from a breeder and make sure the puppy has its own Registration Certificate.

If you don't understand the pedigree, ask if you may make a copy of it and then get someone who is knowledgeable of the breed to explain it to you. The secretary of the relevant breed club should help. Ask the Kennel Club for his or her telephone number. And if you are left in any doubt, don't buy. After all, you are seeking a companion for ten to fifteen years, so it must be the right companion. If there are no litters locally of the breed you want, try the secretary of the breed club or contact the Kennel Club for names and addresses. Two weekly publications, *Our Dogs* and *Dog World*, cover all breeds and carry advertisements of puppies and dogs for sale.

A Puppy Information Pack is available from the Kennel Club. Just quote the breed whose details you require.

Opposite:
Some dogs grow like their owners,
and some owners . . . This young
lad and his pet are clearly well
matched, and enjoy a happy
relationship

preparations for its arrival. During this time it will be weaned but, preferably, remain with its litter companions for a short while after the mother has been removed. This helps puppies to adjust to play and other activities in a family environment, adding to their security and giving a better start in life.

Immunisation of your puppy (and similar protection for the adult dog throughout its life) is most important. Your veterinarian will advise about the best time for this. It is totally irresponsible not to give your dog this protection, as it not only protects your dog but others as well.

A certain amount of immunity is carried to the puppy through the first milk (colostrum) of its mother and this will protect it for a while after birth, but your veterinarian will provide specific protection against distemper, hard pad, hepatitis, parvo-virus and leptospirosis. Annual boosters are also necessary to keep the protection at optimum levels.

PREPARING FOR A NEW DOG

Before your dog or puppy arrives home there are various preparations to be made. Buying a stock of the appropriate food is an obvious one. The second is an adequate, comfortable, warm (but not over heated) bed, in a well-ventilated, light area, free from draughts and damp.

There is a wide variety of beds for dogs and many are designed for hygiene and comfort. You may decide on a basket, but puppies often chew these, so a sturdy, clean cardboard box may be suitable for a start. Whatever you choose, allow for it to last several months. Your dog's bed is an important place for him – where he retires for peace, comfort, and the regular sleep that is so necessary for his healthy survival. It needs to offer a feeling of security as well as comfort. Changing it frequently or moving it around from one site to another will only help to destroy that security.

The bed may need lining, with an old blanket, for example. If you add items such as old clothes, make sure that all buttons etc are removed. If the bed is considerably larger than the puppy, a sausage-shaped 'pillow' made from a large sock stuffed with old clothes makes a useful comforter for the puppy to snuggle up to.

Your puppy should have its own toys, such as hide chews and sterilised bones (available from most pet shops), and perhaps a ball. Balls should be no smaller than a tennis ball. Never use anything like a golf ball which can be unravelled or become lodged in the back of the throat. Old slippers or an unused leather belt are acceptable, but buckles, laces and their metal eyelets, and other trimmings and decorations must be removed first to avoid accidents. Giving a puppy its own possessions to chew will also help prevent it chewing yours!

A feeding dish and drinking water bowl which will belong only to the dog are two more essentials. Buy items which can be scalded with boiling water for cleaning and which are adequate in size for the meals and drinks your dog will enjoy. For detailed advice on feeding, see page 86.

A collar and lead will be needed too. A cheap collar will suffice

Living with children

Children can have fine relationships with dogs providing they understand an animal's needs, reactions and capabilities. The first rule is to remember that a dog is not a child's toy. If a dog or puppy is poked, pulled around, teased or kicked – even in fun – it will become withdrawn, nervous, aggressive or irritable and often ill.

Dogs, like children, need food, sleep and play at regular times; too much or too little of any will be reflected in ill-health, and a child who receives insufficient instruction on how to treat a dog will be neither loved nor trusted by that dog. Train the child to be consistently kind – and to understand the dog – from an early age, and the result will be a firm friendship for life, and consideration for other animals. If the child is very young, the association between dog and child should be supervised by an adult so that both are trained to appreciate the other's feelings and limitations. Owners should also be aware that a child's toys, such as marbles, counters, etc, are potential hazards, especially to a puppy.

Care should be taken to ensure that the puppy is wormed and a veterinarian can advise on good hygienic practices so that the child does not pick up infection from the puppy.

since it will soon be too small, and the second purchase can then be a more elaborate gift if you so wish. The lead should be long enough for you and the dog to walk comfortably together – the length of your arm from finger tips to shoulder is a handy guide. Choke chains are not a good substitute for collars, especially not for young puppies. A longer, training lead is a good idea when you start basic training, from about six months.

Security should be high on the list of important first considerations. Puppies are great escapologists and will tackle even the smallest gap in the garden hedge with vigour, especially if there is a cat or potential playmate on the other side. Check your fences and garden perimeter to make sure that there is no weak point through which a puppy can squeeze. Many puppies are killed on the roads after escaping through garden fences – sometimes endangering the lives of human road users. Ensure also that your gates can be closed, and invest in a large notice which clearly tells visitors, tradesmen etc to 'Please close the gate'. Always check that your garden is secure before letting the puppy out on its own.

You will also need to consider the permitted territory for your dog inside your home. Most dogs hate being confined or restricted to certain rooms in the house though there may be a need for this. The more room available, the better for the dog, though of course you can train your new friend to keep off beds and chairs if you wish. Settle these points before you bring the puppy home so that the whole family can be consistent from the beginning.

If the dog is to be kept in an outside kennel, make sure that there is plenty of space for exercise, that the kennel is weather proof and draught-free, and that there is provision for heating in the cold winter months. The kennel should be sited in a position where it is not subject to extremes of temperature, ie, out of direct sunlight during the heat of the day. It should be adequate in size, ie, high enough for the dog to stand upright without restriction. It should be easy to clean out and bedding should be kept dry at all times.

If you are thinking of confining a puppy to an outside kennel, perhaps the decision to keep a dog should be reviewed. Dogs need companionship. Being left alone in an outside kennel for lengthy periods is unlikely to bring out the best in a dog's character. Never chain a dog up to an outside kennel – in fact, never chain a dog at all. Chained dogs are generally very unhappy creatures, and their neglect often follows automatically. Dogs are not meant to be confined in small spaces, nor chained up.

While a puppy is young, its life consists mostly of sleeping, eating, playing, urinating and defecating. It should be allowed to play and sleep at its own pace, eat at regular specified times, and perform its bodily functions as soon as it needs to do so. Sleep is a vital part of its development and welfare. A puppy should not be woken, therefore, when you (or your family) are ready to play with it; rather you should be ready to play when *it* is ready. While play is a necessary part of learning and personality development, an excessive amount is harmful, causing over-excitement and stress. Children must learn that the puppy is not a toy, that play must never involve any form of teasing, and that the puppy must be allowed to pace the games in its own time and way. When the puppy wants to stop it should be left in peace.

On waking, most puppies need to urinate (at least) immediately and they will have little control over themselves. An alertness on your part will save much trouble for all concerned (see House Training page 55).

A puppy loves to make contact, and it is most helpful to let him sleep safely and undisturbed on your lap for a while if he wishes to do so. Such contact helps to form a strong bond and forge the links of trust and companionship which will last a lifetime.

Healthy puppies are lively and lack control over bladder and bowels at first. They need consistency of command, care and attention. Instruct all members of your family in the patterns you are planning for the newcomer, and do your best to understand its needs.

Playtime

It is very important that you play with your puppy, as he will learn a lot from it. About half-way through a play period a young puppy will stop to do another puddle. If you are outside, say 'Clean dog' as he does it, and 'Good dog' afterwards. If you are playing indoors, look out for the signs; he will start sniffing the floor, so pick him up and take him outside. Always praise a dog when it has done what you want, and never chastise a dog unless you actually catch him in the act of some misdemeanour.

PUPPY TRAINING WITH PHIL DRABBLE

A dog has been my constant companion since I was eight years old; I feel half-dressed without one!

By nature, dogs are predators. It is their instinct not only to find their quarry, but to kill it as well. Only careful training will inhibit this instinct and channel it into useful directions. A lifetime's experience has taught me that it is far easier to prevent bad faults developing than it is to cure them when they have been acquired.

I allow my puppies to come for short walks, in the garden or when I am feeding the poultry, from the age of seven or eight weeks old. At that stage , I can still run faster than they can if a wrong thought enters their heads. I carry a pocketful of whole maize or other corn. By watching intently, it is possible to predict precisely when the puppy is going to fall for the temptation to chase something.

At the instant he starts I deluge him with a handful of corn which rattles round his ears and, at the same time, I rap out the word 'No' – which is the most important word he ever learns. The corn does not hurt him but it distracts his attention so he forgets what it was he had in mind.

By the time they are 12 weeks old (and after their second vaccination), all my puppies are safe and steady with stock without any necessity to strike a blow or speak a word in anger. After that, I shall be proud to be seen in their company because the responsibilities of owning dogs are a small price to pay for the joy they give.

Your dog and the law
The law requires every dog to wear a collar bearing the owner's name and address, whenever the dog is in a public place. The behaviour of dogs on footpaths and other public places is governed by bye-laws which vary with each local authority.

A provision of the Wildlife and Countryside Act 1981 makes it a criminal offence for a dog to be at large in a field or enclosure in which there is livestock, unless he is on a lead or otherwise under close control.

Big dogs run further
If you have a dog of the long-legged variety which needs a good long run to 'let off steam', it is important to select exercise areas where there is no livestock.

If you are in the habit of exercising your dog in town, you will appreciate the need for using a lead. This discipline is just as necessary in the country but to allow your dog a little more freedom, having an alternative country lead is a good idea.

A country lead can be considerably longer than a normal lead, say around ten feet this gives the dog a lot more freedom to run and generally enjoy the countryside. Extending leads can offer a solution to both town and country situations.

EXERCISE

Exercise is vitally important to a dog's welfare, keeping it interested in life and physically and mentally healthy.

Early mornings and evenings are the best times for exercise, especially during the summer months. Apart from heat, the weather rarely affects a dog. Age may take its toll, requiring a slower pace and shorter walks, especially when the weather is wet or cold. A wet dog should always be dried thoroughly on returning home.

Dogs should never be allowed to exercise themselves. Letting a dog out without control is extremely irresponsible – for the rest of society, as well as the dog. Even if a dog has 'road sense', there are many incidents and situations which may result in your dog being killed – or causing an accident which may kill or injure someone else. A male dog left to wander on his own will almost certainly be a nuisance in his quest for female company. In the country, there is the added risk of lone dogs worrying sheep or other stock. If caught in such an act, your dog may be shot by the farmer – quite justifiably. In the town, a stray dog may be stolen, injured, killed, or collected by the police. The risks in both rural and urban areas are very high indeed. Feral dogs – those that have become wild pack animals – cause untold damage, can become vicious and will almost certainly be subject to a life of suffering. A responsible dog owner will never allow his or her dog to roam.

If a dog is given proper exercise, and the security around his home territory is adequate, there is no reason for him to roam. If your male dog becomes troublesome when a local bitch is in season, discuss with your veterinarian the possibility of canine neutering, now a relatively simple procedure which will give owner and dog peace of mind and keep him safer at home.

The amount of exercise depends on the age, size and breed of dog (and, to a lesser extent perhaps, the owner's available time), with young animals needing the most. An hour out, especially if spent running through fields or woods, will suit the average-sized dog, although more is beneficial. If the dog can run free safely without a lead, so much the better. If you are lead walking, a brisk walk is better than a slow stroll. Never run a dog alongside a bicycle or car as the dog cannot pace itself. Apart from the dangers to the dog and to other road users, the practice is injurious to the dog's health.

In pregnancy, gentle, regular exercise is important to keep muscles in trim. In old age the dog should be encouraged to walk at its own pace and distance. Too much energetic exercise, where a dog is pushed beyond the limits of endurance, leads to exhaustion, and can damage the heart.

Exercise should be regular, preferably at the same times each day so that the dog can anticipate and enjoy it. Walks should be planned any time before meals or several hours afterwards, when digestion is complete. Neglect of exercise will inevitably lead to ill health and produce a lethargic, apathetic dog.

Play is not only a part of exercise, utilising surplus energy, perfecting skills and improving muscle control, but it also helps to develop an alert, well-adjusted obedient dog. Throwing a ball or stick for your dog to retrieve will also strengthen the bond between you and your dog. Play with other dogs may include mock aggression or simulated mating. When playing alone, puppies in particular enjoy chewing and manipulating objects around them. Be warned, the things they chew and manipulate will probably be yours! Play is also an important foundation for training puppies. Never play long enough for the puppy to become thoroughly exhausted, nor for it to become bored.

HOUSE TRAINING

House training should begin as soon as the puppy arrives home, though the best age for implementing a full training session for all other commands is between six and twelve months of age. All forms of training should be carried out with firmness, patience, kindness and an understanding of the dog's limitations and capabilities.

House training commences with the understanding that a puppy has little control over itself in its early life, rather like a human baby, though most are anxious to please once they know what you require of them. Puppies need to urinate very soon after they wake from a sleep, and should be hurried outside where they will perform naturally. Praising the puppy at this point helps it to associate the sequence with rewarding words. If it has an accident inside the house, growling words of admonishment have the reverse effect. It really is not much use to scold the puppy unless it is caught in the act. It is never necessary to smack a puppy to house train it. If it is persistent in its misdemeanours, a tap on the body (never the head) with a rolled-up newspaper (if there is one handy) may produce the desired effect. The slapping noise of the paper is really quite loud to a puppy and not at all enjoyable, so it reinforces the scolding action. Most puppies, however, learn from the praising rather than the scolding and respond very quickly. You need to be alert and aim to get the pup to the garden as quickly as you can, thereby eliminating the need for the negative scolding, and for mopping up your carpet! Puppies also need to defecate after a meal and should be accompanied into the garden to observe and congratulate them. You will soon recognise the puppy's pattern and habits.

Walkies

Do not take a three-month-old puppy for a 5 mile walk along mostly main roads unless you want a neurotic, shaking jelly. Always put yourself in the puppy's place – after all, he's a baby, like you once were.

Bones

It is often said that 'dogs in the wild manage all sorts of bones'. Dogs do, indeed, cope with bones of all shapes and sizes but there are no statistics available of the numbers which die as a result of bones becoming lodged in places where they cause stoppage of breath, obstruction of the intestines and many other lethal conditions. The domesticated dog should *never* be fed small, sharp bones (such as chop, rabbit, fish or fowl bones). The risks are considerable and should not be taken. A dog will enjoy (and be safe with) a large beef thigh bone which contains marrow; let the dog chew it for as long as it wants – it is a useful dental cleaner and polisher – and then saw off one end and extract the marrow, which the dog will doubly enjoy. Give the bone raw; cooked bones are less interesting.

Dog Types

Breeding

As man's relationship with his new-found friend developed, so he took in hand the task that up to then had been performed by nature, and developed new breeds to suit his particular purpose. The best example of this is the development of the wolf-like shepherd dog which guarded sheep from their natural prey, the wolf. This dog looked so like a wolf that the predator became wary, as it was not anxious to enter into mortal combat with one of its own kind. In the Greek mountain ranges, sheepdogs were developed that looked like sheep, so that when

continued

We now divide dogs into six groups – Hounds, Gundogs, Toys, Terriers, Working and the rather odd Utility which includes members of all the other groups but classifies them as Non-sporting. The Working group is the largest of the six, followed by Hounds, Gundogs, Terriers, Toys and Utility. The numbers of most of the groups are swollen by some of their members having different sizes and different coat types. For example, the Poodle comes in three different sizes, and the Dachshund comes in both different sizes and different coat types.

HOUNDS

The term is applied to those dogs whose purpose is hunting. Some of the breeds within this group claim ancient lineage. Afghan Hound devotees for example claim Noah took this dog into the Ark. Afghans and Salukis are known to have been in existence in the third millenium BC. The Greeks, Romans and Celts had hounds similar to

The Irish Setter, a beautiful breed

the Deerhound and Greyhound, and the Romans encountered large dogs not unlike the Irish Wolfhound when they conquered Britain.

Some hounds are designed for speed and some for endurance, some hunt by sight and some by scent, some are silent in their pursuit, others vociferous, some kill the prey while others hold the hunted at bay until their masters arrive to strike the final blow.

All hounds have similar characteristics; deep chest, powerful jaws, strong necks, well muscled hindquarters and strong legs and feet. The hound needs to display courage and obedience to command, yet have the ability to work independently.

Hounds generally relate well to humans though some have a stubborn streak of independence of thought and action which can make training a prolonged effort.

GUNDOGS

The purpose of this group of dogs is to drive game from cover, indicate where the birds can be found and to retrieve game that has been shot. They are expected to retrieve game from dense undergrowth, open ground and from water.

continued

the unsuspecting wolf descended on the fold it found itself routed by a vast woolly monster that it had innocently believed to be one of its stupid prey – a veritable wolf in sheep's clothing.

As man became more and more settled in his habits and intellect crept into his life, so there came about a subtle change in his breeding of dogs, and animals such as the Pekinese, the Pug and non-sporting varieties of Spaniel, intended entirely for decoration and companionship, came into being.

Opposite:
A Champion Afghan Hound,
Kaskarak Hitari of Montravia

There are references to spaniels as far back as 1486. All breeds within this group descend from the spaniel family. Originally they were used to drive game into nets but today they work alongside man with his gun.

From the spaniel came the setter, a 'creeping spaniel' reputedly trained by Queen Elizabeth's favourite, Robert Dudley, Earl of Leicester, to find birds and drive them into the net.

The retrievers are the youngest branch; again the spaniel and the setter played a part in their early ancestry.

Gundogs are required to be intelligent, amenable and eager to please. Obedience is essential to avoid the dog being accidentally shot. The gundog is trained to walk slightly back from the heel of his master so that he is always clear of the gun. Many of the gundog breeds make excellent family companions, the most popular being the Golden Retriever and the Labrador Retriever. With their trainability and usually superb temperament they fit well into family life.

TOY DOGS

The fourteen toy dogs familiar to us today have arrived from many different countries as far apart as China, Japan, Malta and Greece. There are some which are dwarf versions of larger breeds. Some miniaturisation came about naturally, some by selective breeding and some by very odd mixtures of feeding herbs, roots and even dosing with the Japanese drink Saki.

The eyes have it! The Yorkshire
Terrier is one of our most popular
toy breeds

Canine campanology

At a convent in France, twenty paupers were served with a dinner at a certain hour every day. A Dog belonging to the convent did not fail to be present at this regale, to receive the scraps which were now and then thrown to him. The guests, however, were poor and hungry, and of course not very wasteful; so that their pensioner did little more than scent the feast of which he would fain have partaken.

The portions were served by a person, at the ringing of a bell, and delivered out by means of what in religious houses is called a *tour*; a machine like the section of a cask, that, by turning round upon a pivot, exhibits whatever is placed on the concave side, without discovering the person who moves it. One day this Dog, which had only received a few scraps, waited till the paupers were all gone, took the rope in his mouth and rang the bell. His stratagem succeeded. He repeated it the next day with the same good fortune. At length the cook, finding that twenty-one portions were given out instead of twenty, was determined to discover the trick; in doing which he had no great difficulty, for, lying in wait, and noticing the paupers as they came for their different portions, and that there was no intruder except the Dog, he began to suspect the truth; which he was confirmed in when he saw the animal continue with great deliberation till the visitors were all gone, and then pull the bell. The matter was related to the community; and to reward him for his ingenuity, the Dog was permitted to ring the bell every day for his dinner, on which a mess of broken victuals was always afterwards served out to him.

Nineteenth-century anecdote

Miniaturisation has invariably brought some changes in conformation by way of shortened limbs, rounded heads and protruding eyes. Most of these can be plainly seen in the popular toy breeds today.

There are references to toy dogs as far back as the fifteenth century when some very curious myths abounded. Dogs were believed to

draw fleas away from humans and the laying of a dog upon a sick person was said to draw away pain and sickness. A small dog was often described as a 'comforter'.

The variety of appearance, character and size makes the toy breeds as popular in our modern homes as they were in palaces and country houses in bygone days.

An English Mastiff bitch and her pup, in suitably regal setting

Penny pie

A grocer in Edinburgh had a
Dog, which for some time
amused and astonished the
people in the neighbourhood. A
man who went through the
streets ringing a bell and selling
penny pies, happened one day to
treat this Dog with a pie. The
next time he heard the pieman's
bell, the Dog ran to him with
impetuosity, seized him by the
coat, and would not suffer him
to pass. The pieman, who
understood what the animal
wanted, showed him a penny,

continued

WORKING GROUP

The name speaks for itself, the dogs within this group all possess
working ability, though many dogs today no longer perform the tasks
for which they were developed. Collies still work sheep and cattle,
and some corgis still work cattle; the German Shepherd is the police
force's choice for many tasks of protection, search and rescue, and
drug finding. Rottweilers are employed by the armed forces, and a
few St Bernards still work in mountain rescue. The working ability
of many breeds is now sadly neglected. The agile, powerful Great
Dane certainly no longer hunts boar and wolf and many of the
modern versions of all working breeds are required to be no more
than attractive examples of their kind.

Most of the working breeds adapt happily to family life and are
devoted and loyal. It should be remembered that they have great
stamina, are mostly large dogs and will need plenty of exercise and
training to occupy their agile minds.

UTILITY GROUP

Dogs in this group represent breeds not developed for any specific
purpose, or breeds whose original purpose has long since disappeared.
This group shows a vast diversity of size and conformation – from the
large and graceful Dalmatian, bred originally as a carriage dog to run
alongside the coaches of the wealthy, to the tiny decorative Tibetan
Spaniel, once a working dog.

The decorative Tibetan Spaniel

TERRIERS

The terriers were the poor relations of the dog world, less pampered than the highly prized hound and yet undoubtedly assisting with hunting, going to ground after foxes and killing rats and other vermin. The name derives from the French 'terre' meaning ground or soil. Fourteenth-century texts and drawings describe 'two sorts – one with crooked legs and a short coat and others with longer legs and shaggy coats'.

These hardy sporting dogs developed into specialised types in various localities throughout Britain. In the nineteenth century the various shapes and sizes became recognised as breeds and most of them were identified by the area from which they came: Yorkshire Terrier, (now a toy breed), Norfolk Terrier, Border Terrier, Manchester Terrier. There is a wide variety of sizes apparent within the Terrier group, ranging from the large Airedale down to the tiny Cairn. Probably the most popular terriers in the home are the Cairn and the West Highland White.

A beautifully groomed Bichon Frisé

continued

and pointed to his master, who stood at the street-door and saw what was going on. The Dog immediately supplicated his master who put a penny into the Dog's mouth, which he instantly delivered to the pieman, and received his pie; and this traffic between the pieman and the grocer's Dog, continued to be daily practised for many months.

Nineteenth-century anecdote

OLD FRIENDS

I looked again at the slip of paper where I had written my visits. 'Dean, 3, Thompson's Yard. Old dog ill.'

There were a lot of these 'yards' in Darrowby. They were, in fact, tiny streets, like pictures from a Dickens novel. Some of them opened off the market place and many more were scattered behind the main thoroughfares in the old part of the town. From the outside you could see only an archway and it was always a surprise to me to go down a narrow passage and come suddenly upon the uneven rows of little houses with no two alike, looking into each other's windows across eight feet of cobbles.

In front of some of the houses a strip of garden had been dug out and marigolds and nasturtiums straggled over the rough stones; but at the far end the houses were in a tumble-down condition and some were abandoned with their windows boarded up.

Number three was down at this end and looked as though it wouldn't be able to hold out much longer.

The flakes of paint quivered on the rotten wood of the door as I knocked; above, the outer wall bulged dangerously on either side of a long crack in the masonry.

A small, white-haired man answered. His face, pinched and lined, was enlivened by a pair of cheerful eyes; he wore a much-darned woollen cardigan, patched trousers and slippers.

'I've come to see your dog,' I said, and the old man smiled.

'Oh, I'm glad you've come, sir,' he said. 'I'm getting a bit worried about the old chap. Come inside, please.'

He led me into the tiny living-room. 'I'm alone now, sir. Lost my missus over a year ago. She used to think the world of the old dog.'

The grim evidence of poverty was everywhere. In the worn out lino, the fireless hearth, the dank, musty smell of the place. The wallpaper hung away from the damp patches and on the table the old man's solitary dinner was laid; a fragment of bacon, a few fried potatoes and a cup of tea. This was life on the old age pension.

In the corner, on a blanket, lay my patient, a crossbred labrador. He must have been a big powerful dog in his time, but the signs of age showed in the white hairs around his muzzle and the pale opacity in the depth of his eyes. He lay quietly and looked at me without hostility.

'Getting on a bit, isn't he, Mr Dean!'

'Aye he is that. Nearly fourteen, but he's been like a pup galloping about until these last few weeks. Wonderful dog for his age, is old Bob and he's never offered to bite anybody in his life. Children can do anything with him. He's my only friend now – I hope you'll soon be able to put him right.'

'Is he off his food, Mr Dean?'

'Yes, clean off, and that's a strange thing because, by gum, he could eat. He always sat by me and put his head on my knee at meal times, but he hasn't been doing it lately.'

I looked at the dog with growing uneasiness. The abdomen was grossly distended and I could read the telltale symptoms of pain; the catch in the respirations, the retracted commissures of the lips, the anxious, preoccupied expression in the eyes.

When his master spoke, the tail thumped twice on the blankets and a momentary interest showed in the white old eyes; but it quickly disappeared and the blank, inward look returned.

I passed my hand carefully over the dog's abdomen. Ascites was pronounced and the dropsical fluid had gathered till the pressure was intense. 'Come on, old chap,' I said 'let's see if we can roll you over.' The dog made no resistance as I eased him slowly on to his other side, but, just as the movement was completed, he whimpered and looked round. The cause of the trouble was now only too easy to find.

I palpated gently. Through the thin muscle of the flank I could feel a hard, corrugated mass; certainly a splenic or hepatic carcinoma, enormous and completely inoperable. I stroked the old dog's head as I tried to collect my thoughts. This wasn't going to be easy.

'Is he going to be ill for long?' the old man asked, and again came the thump, thump of the tail at the sound of the loved voice. 'It's miserable when Bob isn't following me round the house when I'm doing my little jobs.'

'I'm sorry, Mr Dean, but I'm afraid this is something very serious. You see this large swelling. It is caused by an internal growth.'

'You mean . . . cancer?' the little man said faintly.

'I'm afraid so, and it has progressed too far for anything to be done. I wish there was something I could do to help him, but there isn't.'

The old man looked bewildered and his lips trembled. 'Then he's going to die?'

I swallowed hard, 'We really can't just leave him to die, can we? He's in some distress now, but it will soon be an awful lot worse. Don't you think it would be kindest to put him to sleep? After all, he's had a good, long innings.' I always aimed at a brisk, matter-of-fact approach, but the old cliches had an empty ring.

The old man went silent, then he said, 'Just a minute,' and slowly and painfully knelt down by the side of the dog. He did not speak, but ran his hand again and again over the grey old muzzle and the ears, while the tail thump, thump, thumped on the floor.

He knelt there a long time while I stood in the cheerless room, my eyes taking in the faded pictures on the walls, the frayed, grimy curtains, the broken-springed armchair.

At length the old man struggled to his feet and gulped once or twice. Without looking at me, he said huskily, 'All right, will you do it now?'

I filled the syringe and said the things I always said. 'You needn't worry, this is absolutely painless. Just an overdose of an anaesthetic. It is really an easy way out for the old fellow.'

The dog did not move as the needle was inserted, and, as the barbiturate began to flow into the vein, the anxious expression left his face and the muscles began to relax. By the time the injection was finished, the breathing had stopped.

'Is that it?' the old man whispered.

'Yes, that's it,' I said. 'He is out of his pain now.'

The old man stood motionless except for the clasping and unclasping of his hands. When he turned to face me his eyes were bright. 'That's right, we couldn't let him suffer and I'm grateful for what you've done. And now, what do I owe you for your services, sir?'

'Oh, that's all right, Mr Dean,' I said quickly. 'It's nothing – nothing at all. I was passing right by here – it was no trouble.'

The old man was astonished. 'But you can't do that for nothing.'

'Now please say no more about it, Mr Dean. As I told you, I was passing right by your door.' I said goodbye and went out of the house, through the passage and into the street. In the bustle of people and the bright sunshine, I could still see only the stark, little room, the old man and his dead dog.

As I walked towards my car, I heard a shout behind me. The old man was shuffling excitedly towards me in his slippers. His cheeks were streaked and wet, but he was smiling. In his hand he held a small, brown object.

'You've been very kind, sir. I've got something for you.' He held out the object and I looked at it. It was tattered but just recognisable as a precious relic of a bygone celebration.

'Go on, it's for you,' said the old man. 'Have a cigar.'

James Herriot,
All Creatures Great and Small

A friend and companion

One of the chosen is this lucky dog, who is being given a thorough examination in 'friendship' before he leaves Battersea. So often it is not the new owner who chooses a dog, but the dog who makes his own choice in the way he reacts towards them. Here, everything seems all set for a happy relationship to continue in earnest a few yards away on the London pavements

Freddie Reed

Battersea Dogs

TOBY

A mop of hair and a little red nose just peeping over the counter at Reception was my introduction to Jimmy, a five-year-old who had come to report the loss of his pet.

I looked over the top of the counter and said, 'Hello young fellow, what can I do for you?'. Without seeming to pause for breath he replied, 'Please, mister, have you got my pal? He went out and hasn't come home for three days, and I miss him so much. He shouldn't be out, really, and every night I leave my light on so that he can find his way home.' I felt the inevitable lump manifesting itself in my throat as Jimmy went on. 'He's been rather ill with kidney trouble and he hasn't got his pills with him.'

A pause, and the boy's parents stepped forward to report the loss of one black and brown mongrel dog, aged three years, by the name of 'Toby', who had walked out one evening through the garden gate and had not been seen since. They explained that the father had brought his annual holiday forward and they were spending their time following up any clues, however remote, in their search for the missing Toby.

As is the usual practice, a missing dog description form was completed and Jimmy added the information that apart from his

Opposite:
*The tender touch of a child . . .
and the eyes of the dog tell their
own story. They are going to be
great pals – a common occurrence
when a new owner meets his pet,
as yet without a name. Soon these
two were off together to start a
new life somewhere out there:
perhaps they will let us know how
they are getting on, or perhaps
they won't. It would be good
to know.*

Freddie Reed

66

**THE DOGS HOME
BATTERSEA**

Incorporating
The Temporary Home for
Lost and Starving Dogs

4 BATTERSEA PARK ROAD
LONDON SW8 4AA

Telephone: 071-622 3626
Facsimile: 071-622 6451

An Association for the
Protection of Dogs and Cats
A Company Limited by
Guarantee
Registered address as above
No.278802
A Registered Charity No.206394

AIMS AND OBJECTIVES

• To restore lost dogs to their
owners

• To give temporary shelter and
food to lost and starving dogs
and cats

•To provide good homes for
dogs and cats at moderate prices

• To secure a merciful and
painless death for those which
are old, injured, diseased or
dangerous

colour Toby had a broken claw and if you looked closely you would see that he had a few white hairs on his snout, and you would always know him as he could sit and beg and also roll over on command. The lump in the throat was by now excruciatingly painful, eyes were moist, and there were one or two sniffles from the other members of staff present.

In the Home at that time we had 493 dogs of all shapes, sizes and breeds, of which approximately 120 were classified as brown and black mongrel dogs. We offered up a little prayer that one might have a few white hairs on his snout and be able on command to sit, beg and roll over.

The documentation completed, off went the family on a tour of the kennels with Frank, our eagle-eyed keeper, who, if the missing animal was in the Home, would surely find it.

But, alas, half an hour later a tearful Jimmy returned after an unsuccessful search of the kennels. The family said they would call again, and indeed during the following two weeks they paid us a visit nearly every day, always, I was told, at Jimmy's behest. By now all the staff were getting involved and it was no unusual thing to walk around the kennel area and see a young kennel boy with a black and brown new arrival, pleading with it to beg or roll over.

Towards the end of the fortnight we decided to offer Jimmy a replacement for his missing pet. Would he, we asked, care to make his selection from an Alsatian, a St Bernard, a Scottie, or perhaps a Llaso Apso that had been handed in to us because his former master was emigrating. Jimmy was adamant: he wanted no replacement, all he wanted was one black and brown mongrel dog suffering from kidney trouble and answering to the name of Toby.

The boy's parents had by now almost given up any hope they might have had of recovering their son's pet, and their visits to us became more infrequent. During one of these visits I asked them if they had a photo of Toby from which I could get an enlargement made; this they supplied, and we had a blow-up print made which was pinned to the wall in the daily intake area.

By now three months had elapsed, and Jimmy and his missing pet were becoming part of the past, just one of the tear jerkers that occur with unfortunate frequency, and the picture on the wall was faded and tattered. Then our keeper Frank came to me one morning and triumphantly told me that we had now found young Jimmy's missing pet. I couldn't believe it, and when I went along to have a look at one woe begone black and brown mongrel dog I still couldn't believe it was really like the photograph on the wall, although he did sit and beg – but declined to roll over. It was noticed that whoever had taken him into care had scratched the name Prince on his collar.

A telephone call was made to Jimmy's mother and we explained that we had a dog answering Toby's description, although we did suggest that perhaps it would not be right to raise the hopes of her son as it might be a false alarm. She said she would pretend that it was just a normal visit.

Just before the family were due to arrive the dog was leashed to the wall in the kennel area. They say that dogs are almost human, and this little fellow was no exception as he sat there fully alert, seeming to know that at long last he was about to be reunited with his young master. Of course, it just had to be the missing pet.

I escorted the family down when they arrived, Jimmy leading the way. News had got around and the staff on duty were all to be seen at a respectable distance awaiting to see what would happen when Jimmy rounded the corner and came in full view of his missing pet. Recognition was instantaneous: the young master was on his knees cuddling his pet, who for his part howled – could it be at the joy of being reunited with his young master? Our young and not so young kennel staff had a quick whip round, and with the proceeds purchased a new collar and lead and, most importantly, an identity disc. After all the goodbyes, Jimmy and Toby passed out of our lives for ever.

WORLD WAR I

By the time the 1914-18 war broke out, a new block of boarding kennels had been completed at Hackbridge, and were ready just in time to house nearly a hundred working sledge dogs that Ernest Shackleton had sent from Canada, which he intended taking with him on his second Antarctic Expedition. They were all half-breeds, being husky-collie, husky-St Bernard or husky-wolf crosses. Although aloof and with a reputation for savagery, when huskies are domesticated they make excellent companions, growing to love their masters in the same way as other dogs. These huskies of Shackleton's were no exception, for one of the party, Walter How, who died only a few years ago, spoke of the dogs with affection, even remembering some of them individually by name fifty years later.

This enormous, and soon to be famous, pack of dogs was kennelled at Hackbridge for two months completely free of charge, drawing large crowds of sightseers. The field of Antarctic exploration was one that caught the imagination of the general public. One of the Dogs' Home keepers, George Wyndoe, became so expert at handling those large and moderately untamed dogs that he was lent to the

---

Funding

The Home is funded largely by donations from the public, who can become Members or Junior Members, or who leave money to the Home in their wills. Every post brings further donations, some just a few pence, perhaps from an Old Age Pensioner or a child who has saved his pocket money.

A suitable clause for your Will

'My trustees shall retain cash or investments equal at the time of such retention to £X and apply the whole or any part of the capital or income thereof for the benefit, upkeep, maintenance, grooming and proper exercise of my dog . . . , during the rest of his life, and for his decent burial thereafter, and any unexpended part of the said £X shall form part of my residuary estate.'

expedition to escort the greater number of dogs on the first leg of their journey as far as Buenos Aires.

George Wyndoe had had a chequered career. Before he joined the staff at Hackbridge he had travelled from fairground to fairground, all over Britain selling patent medicines. On some occasions he had been obliged to beat a hasty retreat, when after a particularly successful day's sales he had taken to replenishing his supplies with ordinary tap water. He had 'the gift of the gab', and remained in the employ of the Home until his retirement; and even then he came back regularly to collect his pension and regale his old friends with tall stories.

REBEL

David was going through the typically rebellious adolescent stage of running away from home, and being repeatedly suspended from his grammar school. After a major row with his parents, he packed a rucksack and, with £12 in his pocket, headed for Battersea, because he'd always wanted a dog. He emerged from the Home half an hour later having acquired a fellow adolescent; a huge but emaciated sandy mongrel, who'd come up to the bars and licked his hand. He named the dog Rebel. It had cost him, including collar and lead, £11.50. Together they trekked to Roehampton, where David's last 50p went on a bottle of pop and a packet of crisps which Rebel shared. The dog was obviously ravenous, but never once during the long day did he growl or grumble, but just kept walking close to David's side, occasionally licking his hand to reassure him. By one o'clock in the morning they were both exhausted, and decided to bed down under a tree. 'Feeling this big friendly animal by my side,' writes David, 'I started wondering how I was going to feed him, then I thought of my parents and how worried they must be, went straight to a telephone box, and rang home. I told them I'd got a big dog. They were so relieved they wouldn't have minded an elephant. My father came and picked us up, and fell in love with Rebel at once.'

Rebel's troubles however were not over. Next day it was plain that he had distemper. He nearly died. The entire Bellett family joined forces to save his life, nursing him all round the clock. Happily he pulled through. After such communal achievement, David patched up his differences with his parents, and is now happily working as a French polisher.

PIP

The well-known photographer and big-game hunter of the nineteen-twenties, Cherry Kearton, bought a small Fox Terrier for 7/6d from the Dogs' Home that was destined to win the coveted prize of a lion's mane when it was on safari in Africa.

Kearton visited the Home to find a small dog to take with him as a companion on an expedition that he was planning. '. . . She had a silly little stump of tail, which began to wag as soon as she saw me. I stood in front of her kennel and laughed; the tail wagged faster than ever.'

Greyfriars Bobby

The most celebrated example of mongrel devotion, of course, is Greyfriars' Bobby, the Romney Marshall owned by a Midlothian farmer called Gray. Every week Gray and Bobby came to Edinburgh on market day, and lunched at a restaurant in Greyfriars called Traill's where Bobby was given a large bun as a special treat. Gray died in 1858 and was buried in Greyfriars churchyard. A few days later, Mr Traill was upset to see an emaciated, starving Bobby slink into the restaurant. On being offered one of his favourite buns, the dog snatched it and bolted. After several such visits, Mr Traill trailed Bobby and found him wolfing the bun on his master's grave. On hearing this, neighbours tried to offer the dog a home, but Bobby always escaped back to the grave, huddling under a tombstone for warmth when the weather became too severe. In the end, he became a national institution. The people of Greyfriars built a shelter near the grave, which he never deserted except to collect his buns, which were the only food he would touch. On such a diet he lived another fourteen years and was buried beside his master.

What an incredible change it must have been for this little dog that had known only the streets of London to find herself in the wilds of Africa. The purpose of the expedition was to photograph lions in their natural habitat, a most difficult and dangerous occupation in those days long before Land Rovers and game reserves.

Pip was to prove a dauntless and tenacious little animal. One day news was received at the camp that there were two man-eating lions at large near a native village, so Kearton set off armed only with his camera, accompanying eleven young Maasai warriors with spears. Four Somali horsemen rode forward as scouts, to try to entice the

Most dogs are anxious and eager to please

Cindy the Jack Russell

Perhaps the most remarkable mongrel survivor was Cindy, a small Jack Russell who made the television news when she got trapped in a mine shaft. Miners tried for days to reach her, as did the police, the fire brigade and the local RSPCA. Her pitiful cries grew weaker and weaker, and after much heart searching it was decided the only way to prevent her dying slowly of starvation was to blow her up with dynamite. This was done, and her cries were heard no more. Sadly, her would-be-saviours returned home. Imagine their amazement, several hours later, when Cindy suddenly turned up at her own home, thinner, dirty, but alive and well. The explosion had loosened the rock where she was imprisoned, so she was able to dig through what was left and emerge in a totally different part of the hillside. Fortunately Jack Russells have an excellent sense of locality and she found her way home in no time.

lions to come closer. The young Maasai warriors formed themselves into a crescent-shaped line, but, just as they were advancing slowly and cautiously, Pip appeared suddenly at Kearton's side, very excited and eager not to be left out of the fun. A moment later, the party came face to face with the two lions, furiously angry, snarling and tearing at the earth with their forepaws, a terrifying sight. Attack after attack by the spearmen failed, as they could not get near enough to their prey to sink their spears into them. At last the lions bounded off, but the trackers knew that one of them was lying hidden somewhere not far away. Then Kearton had a brainwave. He wondered whether Pip might help, and loosed her hoping that she would use her nose to mark the animal, and by her shrill barks would enable the spearmen to move swiftly, close in and finish it off. Pip, ever eager for action, dashed off and, to everyone's amazement, dived into the dried-up bed of a stream and disappeared. That instant there came a terrible roar from the very place where Pip had vanished, and minutes later it was all over. The lion lay dead, but there also was Pip, still growling and holding the lion's tail firmly clenched between her teeth. She had distracted its attention, giving a warrior the opportunity to creep up and thrust his spear straight through the beast's heart. But, as he did so, Pip had rushed round and sunk her teeth into the tail, utterly refusing to let go.

It is the custom with the Maasai tribe that the man who takes the lion's tail is entitled to its mane – a great triumph and honour. So there was this dauntless little Battersea stray laying claim to the mane of a man-eating lion and earning for herself the nickname of 'Simba', the lion.

AIRDALE JACK

In the British War Museum is a small wooden stand . . . to the memory of Airdale Jack, a hero of the Great War.

Just a dog . . . but a hero who in 1918 saved a whole British battalion from being annihilated by the enemy.

Airdale Jack was sent over to France as a messenger and guard. There was a big push on, and he was taken by the Sherwood Foresters to an advance post.

The battle raged, and things went badly against the Foresters. The enemy sent across a terrific barrage, cutting off every line of communication with headquarters, four miles behind the lines.

It was certain that the entire battalion would be wiped out unless reinforcements could be secured from headquarters, but how? It was impossible for any man to creep through the walls of death that surrounded them.

But there was just one chance – Airdale Jack. Lieutenant Hunter slipped the vital message into the leather pouch attached to the dog's collar. A pat on the head and then simply: 'Goodbye, Jack . . . Go back, boy.'

The battalion watched Jack slip quietly away, keeping close to the ground and taking advantage of whatever cover there was, as he had been trained to do.

The bombardment continued, and the shells fell all around him. A piece of shrapnel smashed the dog's lower jaw . . .but he carried on. Another missile tore open his tough, black and tan coat from shoulder to haunch – but on he went, slipping from shell-crater to trench.

With his forepaw shattered, Jack had to drag his wounded body along the ground for the last three kilometres. There was the glaze of death in his eyes when he reached headquarters but he had done a hero's work and saved the battalion.

Jack, a Battersea dog, was presented with a posthumous VC.

Sasha escaped from her owner through a hole in the garden fence . . . and just kept walking. A reunion such as this is just another part of the good life at Battersea, when a pet is safe in the arms of its owner once more. Am I glad to see you!

Freddie Reed

SUSIE

Another triumph for Bitches' Lib was Susie of Battersea. Anyone who visited the Home until a few years ago would have been surprised to see a little black and white Family Circler called Susie charging about as though she owned the place. Susie's story is a sad one which ended happily. For many years she was the devoted companion of an old lady who finally, at the age of eighty-two, set fire to her bed by accident in the middle of the night. Susie promptly raised the alarm by barking her head off, and saved the old lady's life by tugging the burning sheets and blankets off her bed.

The old lady recovered in hospital, and agreed to go to an old people's home, but was terribly distressed about abandoning Susie. She was only comforted when Battersea informed her that the bitch would end her days in the Home as official guard dog. Susie soon attached herself to one of the keepers and made herself very useful by rounding up any dog that got loose, and barking until a member of the staff returned it to its pen. She reached a good age before she died one night in her sleep.

BORIS OF BATTERSEA

Boris was purchased complete with lead for £30.80p on 1 October 1987. He does not have any name recorded on the invoice, only a registered No 13645, is described simply as a black and brindle dog. His keeper was No 9.

Boris became a travelling companion and guard for his new owner, who had built a large 'house' on the back of a huge rugged Mercedes Truck. During the months that followed, Boris travelled thousands of miles overland through many counties, but mostly across Africa and finally to Kenya, where this intrepid and by now experienced overlander spent several very happy months by the Indian Ocean, enjoying the fun of chasing the crabs and seabirds along the lovely beaches and socialising with other travellers and local residents. Everybody knew Boris, a much loved character.

Worming procedures

Puppies should be wormed at about three to four weeks of age, and again at two months and three months. Thereafter worming should be carried out at four to six monthly intervals. Watch the dog's faeces (and the hair around the anus where worm traces can be seen) for any signs of internal parasites so that worming can be done quickly. Proprietary worming tablets are available with dosage according to weight of dog marked on the packaging. These are normally quite palatable and can be easily fed by hand or mixed with the dog's food. While some tablets are active collectively against roundworms and hookworms, a specific medicament will generally be needed to eliminate tapeworms. If in doubt contact a veterinarian.

Bitches should be dosed before mating and after whelping. Sick dogs should not be dosed without clearance from a veterinarian.

Boris of Battersea

Alas, the day came when his owner had to sell the caravan and fly back to England. He could not visualise Boris having to serve at least six months confined in a quarantine kennel, quite apart from the huge cost of a crate and airfreight for a big dog weighing some 70lb (about 32 kilos). A suitable and permanent home was urgently needed.

People in this area know that I am an advisory director with WSPA and work for animal welfare internationally, so I was duly contacted. I had lost my dog when he and several others were poisoned around Christmas time, but I was reluctant to take in a dog at that time as I was planning to go on leave soon. However, several very unsuitable people were interested in acquiring a large 'guard-dog' cheaply, so to save Boris from a miserable life living on the end of a chain, I took him there and then.

The day he came to me he was obviously a very sick dog. His owner thought that maybe it was just that the dog had sensed he was leaving him and was pining. I took him straight to my vet, who found he had a very high temperature and feared he might be suffering from a fatal disease transmitted by the tsetse fly, which is rampant along the coast. Blood tests, however, showed that he had *Ricketsiosis Ehrlicia Canis,* a tick-borne disease. For a couple of days his life was in real danger, but luckily he responded to treatment and finally came home, a weakened shadow of his former self, but he is now a big healthy dog once more.

My little spayed African dog had missed her other playmate desperately, so she was delighted with the arrival of Boris and I am certain played a big part in helping him settle into his new home, where we hope he will live happily ever after.

Juanita Carberry
Kenya

BIG BRUNO

We chose our wonderful dog a month ago from the Home, and already we just would not part with him! He is faithful, protective, a bit naughty sometimes – in fact, just part of the family. We have named him Bruno (after Frank!) as he acts fierce, but is just a big softy underneath.

Mary Smyth

One of the gang

Sometimes a dog becomes the communal pet of many children. Laddie, a Borderline Collie, went to school every day at Linskill High School, North Shields. At the end of term he was presented with a certificate by the headmaster commending him for punctuality and good attendance. The whole school cheered as he was led on to the platform. Battersea Dogs' Home also remembers an incident a few years ago, when two very scruffy small boys rolled up at the Home, asking for the immediate return of their mongrel who'd been picked up by the police. They were from the Isle of Dogs, they said, and the dog was a stray – who'd been adopted by their gang of about forty boys, and who slept each night in a different house belonging to a member of the gang. Why had the police nicked the dog, they complained bitterly, when it was minding its own business?

'Why didn't you tell the police it was your dog?' asked the man on the gate.

'We didn't like to say anyfink,' said the scruffier of the two boys, 'because we 'adn't got 'im a licence.'

'But we've 'ad a whip-round and bought one,' said his mate, waving an already dirty and crumpled piece of paper.

Happily the dog soon afterwards turned up at the Home and was joyfully reunited with the gang of forty.

DAISY

A few days before Christmas, thirteen years ago, I came to the Home to choose my Christmas present. A present I had asked for, wheedled, pleaded and begged for, over the previous two years.

I was twenty-seven years old, a van delivery driver, and had been living with my boyfriend Colin in Ilford for the past two years. Always having had a dog when I lived at home, I now felt lost without one and knew that the company I worked for would not mind me taking a dog out in the van with me. My only stumbling block to obtaining a dog was Colin's reluctance to have one, and I felt it was important that he agreed to it as well. Finally he relented, and came with me to select my long-awaited present.

I had always vowed that I would get a dog from a rescue centre, feeling it immoral to buy a dog from a shop or a breeder when there are so many needing homes. I also wanted one I felt would not easily obtain a home but, on a practical level, one that was still young enough to train out any bad habits and small enough to be comfortable riding around in a van. And preferably a dog, not a bitch.

On entering the Home and viewing the dogs my excitement soon turned to despair: so many piteous sights, cowering in corners, yapping frantically, staring resignedly, sleeping uncaringly. Young ones, old ones, scarred, scared and mistreated ones. They all swam before my eyes as I cried and cried in pity and anger that they should be there at all.

Colin was embarrassed at my loud, hiccuping sobs and strode in front down aisle after aisle, passing me tissues and imploring me to 'pick one so we can get out of here'. One dog caught my eye, it looked young (five months), and as though it would not grow into a large dog (small head and feet). It sat quietly and stoically in a cage and was probably one of the most unattractive looking dogs I had ever seen, with a rough, sandy coat sticking up in all directions and a wispy beard around the mouth. It was a bitch and not a dog, so I continued my search until I had seen and cried for them all.

The ugly mongrel bitch stayed in my mind, so in the end I chose her (£6, please). Colin could not believe it! 'It's 'orrible'. 'Why can't we get a proper dog?' He had been eyeing the 'butch' dogs, Alsatians and Dobermanns, but I knew she filled all my requirements except one and I could soon get her spayed and cure that.

Whilst she was taken from the cage, walked to reception, looked over by the vet, and the sold form was completed, she stood quietly on the lead. A canine picture of a well-behaved dog – until we reached the street. When the Home's doors shut behind her she went berserk, spinning in circles, yapping and pulling in all directions. I dragged this lunatic into the car and there we had to sit for twenty minutes, while she leapt from one lap to another, licking frantically. Colin looked as nervous and resigned as some of the inmates had earlier, but I thought it was only temporarily excited behaviour and she would calm down later. She did – one *year* later.

We went through all the trauma of ripped wallpaper, carpets, shoes, and much more. We even stopped her disconcerting habit of running along the back of the settee and sitting on our heads, leaving her tail dangling between our eyes. She was taken to training school each week and came to work with me each day, where she quickly took on the roll of guard dog, allowing only me to enter the van. This did not prevent her taking sweets, biscuits and strokes through the passenger window from a large variety of regular friends and any passing trade who was sucker enough. My pleas to stop feeding her, as it was ruining her figure and would lead to damage to her teeth, met with outward agreement. Now I never saw anyone near the van, but when I entered it she would be lying in a nest of crumbs with a bloated and smug look about her. Daisy (after the dog-daisy weed), as I had named her, became part of the firm and my family.

The next few years passed with Daisy turning into a well behaved adult dog, who had mercifully grown into her bizarre looks. Then in my thirtieth year Colin and I decided to get married and have a family. Shortly before my thirty-first birthday, I had a son, Rhys, and was now concerned how Daisy would react to the new member of the family. Would she be jealous, spiteful? I had asked a nursing sister, who ran the ante-natal clinic, what I should do with my new baby, 'old' dog situation. Luckily she was a 'doggy' person and advised that I should introduce the baby to the dog immediately I brought him home. The child would smell of me, and whilst Daisy smelt him all over I should make encouraging noises and stroke her. She said I should never banish the dog from the room in the first few weeks when I was attending to the baby, but should let the dog observe and therefore know that this was the new 'pup', and she would naturally accept her new place in the family pecking order. I took her advice and she was right – too right! Daisy's van-guarding duties, now defunct, turned to the baby and the pram. For the first few weeks only Colin and I were allowed to touch him directly. If a visitor wanted to hold him, one of us had to pick him up and hand him to the visitor. Daisy would then sit and glare menacingly until he was safely returned.

Less than two years later Laura was born, the process was repeated and Daisy now had two 'pups' to look after – and look after them she did! Many times I had to apologise, to people who would peer into the pram or pushchair, for the nip on the leg they would sustain if I was not there immediately to give them permission to do so and to stand there while they did. We became a regular feature of the nearby shops, parks and forests. I was either pushing a pushchair, with Daisy tied to it; or the two kids were toddling on in front with Daisy circling around them, 'seeing off' any dog that tried to get near; or the children were standing at the edge of the pond, floating a stick or throwing stones, with Daisy pacing up and down behind them, not allowing dog or person to come near in case the kids got knocked into the water.

During this time I started a part-time job with a childminder, and one of my duties was to pick up children from playgroup and school several times a week. Of course, I took Daisy for the exercise on these occasions. The children would take it in turns to hold her lead and walk her back, and she could be trusted with the smallest. The trouble was that all these children then became her extended family and would come under her 'protection' when we took them for outings to the seaside, parks, forests. At these times, when there could be twenty children, Daisy would run from front to back and side to side barking at them, to herd them into a manageable group. God help the child who tried to stray! She was a great help to the childminder and myself, and the children accepted her 'herding' more than any calls and shouts from us not to go too far ahead or wander off to the side.

Daisy's good sense and courage were remarkable, and there are too many instances to list here. She became quite a local character, always seen at playgroup and school, waiting with me for members of her 'family'. Colin once complained that when waiting outside playgroup with the dog, everyone came up to or called out to Daisy, and ignored him completely! Through our daily walks she was well known in the parks, and I made many friends that way.

Once again the years drifted by, with Rhys and then Laura starting playgroup, infant school, juniors, and before I knew it Rhys was nine, Laura seven, I was forty and Daisy was thirteen. Just before her thirteenth Christmas with us she had a fit. I took her to the vet, left her there for tests and came back later, to be told that she had had several more, was now totally blind and had a large brain tumour. They advised me to have her destroyed. Of course, I agreed, and stayed with her while it was administered. Then came the awful task of telling family and friends, local kids, park-walking friends, shopkeepers and the

'Sssh! Listen, the lawyer's about to tell them I've left it all to the Battersea Dogs' Home.'

childminder's kids. Like all bereavements, there is a lot of crying at first, then it gets less, and gradually one gets used to the loss.

Last week I was looking after some children for the childminder. I told them to put on their coats and we would go for a walk in the park. The others were aware of Daisy's death, but the two-year-old looked around, puzzled. 'Where Daisy?' he asked. 'Daisy gone', I replied. He looked thoughtful for a moment before pronouncing 'Get more Daisy' as the answer to the problem. But I will get no more Daisy, at least until I retire. I will be going back to work full-time soon and the chances of finding another job that will let me bring a dog along must be slim; I simply do not believe in leaving a dog alone all day.

I have written Daisy's story because after Christmas there was the usual item from Battersea Dog's Home on television on unwanted pets that had already been abandoned, and I felt that those who work there must get pretty depressed about humanity and its inhumanity to dogs. So I thought it would be nice if I wrote a story on one of its previous inmates who led a full, happy life and gave a great deal of pleasure to those who were lucky enough to have bought her from the Home. So keep up the good work, because in twenty years' time I want to come there again to buy my retirement dog. Thanks a lot all at Battersea.

Jean Walters

DUSTY ON HOLIDAY

Here is Dusty enjoying himself in the sea. We got him from Battersea about three years ago and we now think of him as one of the family – he comes on holiday with us in our camper!

M. Walkling

Jacky

A typical example of the pre-war Terrier mongrel was Jacky Bowyer-Kairns, an adorable, mournful-eyed, brown and white Hover Cur found wandering through Bradford without a collar. Once shown a trick, Jacky knew how to do it. When told to shut the door, he immediately stood on his hind legs and banged it shut with his front paws. He would always bring the post upstairs when it arrived, and rush off down-stairs to fetch the dustpan and brush if anything needed sweeping up.

'His praying was wonderful too,' writes Mrs Bowyer-Kairns. 'A sweet was placed on a stool, and Jacky would kneel well down on his front paws, one eye closed, the other open. Then you said, "Please make Jacky a good boy, let him go to heaven with his friends when he dies", and so on as long as you wanted until, at the magic word Amen, he would gobble up the sweet.'

A LETTER FROM CLEOPATRA

Dear Friends

I am sorry to have taken so long to thank you for taking care of me when I visited your establishment some time ago. If I didn't eat or wag my tail, it's just that I didn't fully appreciate all you were doing for me when I was lost and lonely.

On 9 January 1984 I was taken to my new home in South London. I must admit that I was a bit naughty at first. I was so hungry after my hunger-strike that I jumped up on the table and stole a joint of roast beef when they weren't looking. I was so ashamed when they told me off. I enjoyed the roast beef dinner but decided not to do that any more.

At night, when I was shut in the kitchen with my own carpet and bed, I used to knock over the rubbish bin – not to look for food, but to tell everyone about my unhappiness at being alone. A couple of serious talks and finger-waggings failed to make any impression on me, so my family decided to leave the door open and let me wander and sleep wherever I liked. I can honestly say that I have never done anything wrong from that day to this.

One problem that I encountered was an elderly Siamese cat who was already in residence. Nevertheless, we decided that we could live together amicably, and did so until February 1988, when the poor old boy died of old age. I missed him, and I moped about a bit until, to my surprise, he was replaced by a very elegant (and very lively) youngster. I soon gave him the low-down on how to exist with humans and have a good time. I also trained him to behave himself, and often had to take his head in my mouth in the early days. I was named Cleopatra, after the beautiful Egyptian queen, so the cat was called Caesar.

Our family suddenly decided to move – not just round the corner,

GETTING THE HANG OF SNOWY

Snowy is now an established part of our family. She came from you last April and, despite a very tearful phone call from me a week later, I managed to get the hang of letting her 'know who's master' and she's now a lovely, easy dog. I wanted to let you know how well it all worked out, as it must be so easy to get depressed in your job with the number of homeless dogs. Many thanks, keep up the good work.

Claire Munday

but to Spain! There were many visits to my friend the vet for inspections and injections. (I love everyone in a white coat, even if they do stick things in me.) Sadly, my friend Caesar climbed over the fence and was run over a few weeks before we were due to fly to our new home.

In September 1988 we all went to Heathrow. My boss told me to walk into a little box. Terrible things happened after that, and when he took me out of the box in Alicante, I wouldn't speak to him for several minutes.

We stayed for a few months in a lovely place where I had the run of the countryside and all the company I needed. Local dogs came to visit me, and we went for walks, and sometimes we chased the wild cats away to some other territory, so we wouldn't be kept awake at night by their fights and serenades.

In February we at last moved into our own villa here in Javea. We have beautiful views over the bay and the mountains, and the air is so fresh and clean. My family say that I am The Best Dog in the World. I know this, but it's not becoming to be too conceited. Now we have settled I am ready to take on the responsibilities of being a mother again – so I now have a tiny Spanish Siamese kitten to lick into shape. He is only ten weeks old, but he understands that I can help him, and as I was helped in the past, the least I can do is to help my fellow creatures.

Many thanks for caring for me in my early days – I can recommend your service to all. Now I have to go and play ball in the garden with my family, so I must close.

Thank you, from a very grateful client.

Cleopatra
(as telepathised to Rosemary Hill)

Sappho

Sappho Steffans, a Black and Tan Tightskin with pixie ears, knew what she wanted in life. Intensely friendly, she loved sticking her head through the garden gate to be stroked by the local children. One day her master and mistress decided the gate was falling to pieces, and came home with a new wrought-iron one. None of them could understand Sappho's violent disapproval, as she ran around barking furiously.

'She doesn't like the new gate,' said the youngest child suddenly. At which Sappho seemed to nod, put her nose through the new gate, and then rushed enthusiastically back to the old gate which was lying on the lawn. Suddenly everyone realised she couldn't get her head through the new gate, and, feeling slightly foolish, they took dog and gate back to the shop, and asked for one that fitted. The moment they were shown a gate with wider spaced bars, Sappho shoved her head through and barked her approval.

Criminal case

In the year 1791, a person went to a house in Deptford, to take lodgings, under pretence that he had just arrived from the West Indies; and, after having agreed on the terms, said he should send his trunk that night, and come himself the next day. About nine o'clock in the evening, the trunk was brought by two porters and was carried into a bedroom. Just as the family were going to bed their little house-dog, deserting his usual station in the shop, placed himself close to the chamber-door, where the chest was deposited, and kept up an incessant barking. The moment the door was opened, the Dog flew to the chest, against which it scratched and barked with redoubled fury. They attempted to get the Dog out of the room, but in vain. Calling in some neighbours, and making them eye-witnesses of the circumstance, they began to move the trunk about; when they quickly discovered that it contained something that was alive. Suspicion becoming very strong, they were induced to force it open; when, to their utter astonishment, they found in it their new lodger, who had thus been conveyed into the house with the intention of robbing it.

Nineteenth-century anecdote

Distemper

Canine distemper is a serious virus disease which attacks the nervous system of dogs, foxes and members of the Mustelidae family, including badgers, ferrets, stoats and mink. It is highly infectious, especially among young dogs, although it can be contracted by dogs of all ages. Those between three and twelve months are the most vulnerable.

continued

TWO DELIGHTFUL DOGS

We are truly delighted with the two dogs we took from Battersea last year. The dogs chosen by us are bitches, one a 'slim-line' brindle and the other a powerful black Labrador cross, now named Flora and Emma respectively. They settled into our home very quickly, and apart from the kennel-cough (now cured) and the odd inevitable puddle, they are great in the house and adore my mother who, of course, spoils them dreadfully. They have accepted our cats but will give chase if they run, and they have a good bark at neighbouring dogs.

They are improving on the lead but do tend to go berserk if a dog or cat appears. In the park they are very good and will return when called – unless they are busy chasing other dogs, squirrels, rooks or anything else that dares to move! However, they are responding to training and I'm sure will be fine in a few months.

Thank you, once again, for all your help and for letting us have these two gorgeous dogs. Incidentally, they get on extremely well with my son's two ex-Battersea dogs.

Jane Langford

A 'THOROUGHBRED MONGREL'

I had my dog Pippa from Battersea twelve years ago. She knows everything I am thinking and I call her my 'thoroughbred mongrel'. She is fed on beef and she tells me to curry the chicken; for a treat she has a tin of 'Chummy'. My doctor says having Pippa was the best thing I could have done. She has her injections every year and is very well.

She is famous in our town because she goes to Church with me at least three time a week: when we stand up so does she, and when we kneel she puts her head down between her paws.

She is adorable and so pretty, I love her. I hope I will have her a long time yet. When I am in hospital she goes to a friend who loves her – she never goes into kennels.

Thank you for giving me such a lovable dog.

Beatrice Watts (age 78)

LOVELY LUCY

I am one of those people who used to be absolutely terrified of dogs – in fact, if one appeared in the distance, I would go rigid and change my direction. My son and daughter always wanted a dog, but we had two cats so (fortunately) it was out of the question.

However, at the age of twenty my son became engaged, and because his fiancée lived with her sister he saw a way of having a dog in their house! One morning he and his young fiancée told me of their plan, and the very excited couple travelled to the Home to choose a dog. Apparently they were deeply moved by the number of animals who needed homes and did their 'little party piece' to try to cajole people into wanting them. To my horror they were looking for a large dog, but I had told them that as long as I didn't see it that was up to them. There was one particular dog – a cross between a collie and Alsatian – which was described by Battersea as having 'a lovely nature', and the first thing they did was to find a name for her before she even left the Home. Because she responded immediately to 'Lucy', that was what they chose.

Can you imagine my distress when Lucy was brought, on a lead, to meet me? 'Keep that thing away from me – take it *out!*' (Poor Lucy!). I think she settled fairly well with the two girls, and of course our son saw her a great deal.

However, the friendship between the youngsters began to get a bit 'stormy', and one evening I came back home to find Lucy blissfully sleeping in front of our fire, and one extremely outraged cat who hadn't even managed to be noticed by this great imposter. The engagement was off and we would have Lucy. 'Oh no, we won't' I said. 'So what do we do then, have a healthy animal put to sleep?', said my husband.

That was Sunday evening. On Monday my husband, daughter and son made a *great* fuss about cuddling Lucy and whispering into her ear: 'Remember *everything* we have told you – Mummy's terrified, *please* be gentle,' and left me with her while they went to work. I looked at her sometimes while I worked, and washed the kitchen floor, which she did not attempt to walk on while it was wet – I was pretty amazed about that. In the middle of the morning I had a cup of tea with a biscuit, whereupon Lucy appeared again and quietly sat next to me, gazing into my eyes with the most amazing love I had ever seen in any animal. I held out a biscuit for her and, to my surprise, she moved her head towards my hand very, very slowly and gently took the biscuit from me. I looked into her eyes again and she sighed with a deep love as she looked at me.

When my worried family came home wondering whether I had survived my terrible ordeal, I said, 'Don't ask me today – it's not possible for any animal to behave like she has for more than one day'.

After four days I had taken her out for a walk and discovered that I was going out with a wonderful friend who loves life and comes immediately when called. It took me just those four days to become completely entranced by Lucy, but the thing that really 'melted' me was that she absolutely adored me, when I could not love her.

Now, after three years, our lovely Lucy must know all our personal secrets as we 'confide' in her. (I think she has sometimes licked away tears of sadness from my daughter when she has opened her heart to her.) Lucy takes care of our twenty-year-old cat and licks her if she hasn't managed to wash some neglected areas. She plays with the younger cat if he comes for a game, or gives him a lick of affection when he wants love. She knows how to keep out of our way when we are busy. In the mornings she comes and looks at each one of us, but will not attempt to wake anyone who is still asleep.

I thought you might be interested to hear about the whereabouts of one of your past dogs. I feel I want to thank you from the bottom of my heart.

Maureen Longman

continued

Symptoms include a rise in temperature and a thickening discharge from nostrils and eyes. The dog becomes lethargic, depressed and loses interest in food. Respiratory complications may arise (including cough, bronchitis and severe bronchopneumonia) or those of intestinal origin (including diarrhoea, vomiting and abdominal infection), depending on secondary attack by bacteria. In some forms of the disease the pads of the feet become swollen, thick and hard, a condition known as 'hard pad'. Nervous conditions may also be present, especially in the later stages and sometimes convulsions occur with following paralysis.

Distemper is better prevented than treated since treatment is rarely effective and the disease often proves fatal. Even if the dog is lucky enough to recover through the use of medication followed by extreme care in convalescence to prevent rapid relapse, complications may arise in later life. Immunisation at ten to twelve weeks of age provides protection and regular boosters are advisable. No puppy should be allowed in public prior to its immunisation for fear of contracting distemper (or other serious diseases such as hepatitis and leptospirosis).

Widespread immunisation in the past has substantially contributed to the rarity of distemper in modern times. Never accept that a puppy or dog has been immunised unless supported by a certificate signed by a veterinarian. If in doubt, arrange for the immunisation to be carried out as soon as possible.

WELL-TRAVELLED TOBY

My son and I have been so happy with our little Sheltie Toby, who we rescued from the Home just a year after having to have our fourteen-year-old Rough Collie put to sleep. Toby goes every weekend to Eastbourne, which he loves, and we are going away to north Wales soon: I wonder if he will remember last year's holiday there?

Toby cries when my son is unable to take him to work, it's a real little cry from his heart, so I cuddle him and say Geoffrey won't be long. He really is a little dear. My daughter has four dogs from the Home and we take him to her house each week. At first he was rather undecided about this little 'family' as she actually has all small dogs, but Toby is getting used to them gradually – he really is very well behaved.

Mrs White

BATHING BEAUTIES

These are the two bitches (not very close, I'm afraid) which we had from you three years ago, playing in the sea. I have shown them in local exemption shows and won prizes,and although they were a bit mad when we had them, we are doing quite well in the training/obedience competitions. I bought them as Labrador crosses, but have since been told they are probably Flat Coated Retriever/ Labrador first crosses. Flat Coated Retrievers are almost unknown in this part of the country, so Sheba, the long-haired bitch, always raises a few questions when I take her walking or to a show.

Mrs L. Jones

A LETTER FROM RUSTY

I would like to introduce myself to you. For the last twelve years I have been called Rusty. My family came and chose me from Battersea on 14 December 1977. You and my local vet determined that I was approximately eighteen months old, which now makes me thirteen-and-a-half!

I am loved, always well looked after and well fed. I have regular visits to my vet and have never had anything seriously wrong with me. People say I look young for my age, as my coat is well groomed, with a nice sheen.

I go out for a walk twice a day and often go to the woods for a run. For my part, I try to repay my family by being a good house dog and often hear them say that I am! I live with my master, mistress and their two, now grown-up daughters. In May this year a Sealyham puppy called Monty came to live with us as well. We get on well together and he joins me on my walks.

Well, thank you for looking after me while I was at Battersea. I enclose a photograph of myself. I expect you won't remember me, but this is what I look like now. I am a first cross collie/Basset hound, and have a lovely temperament.

Yours in happy retirement,
Rusty (and the Lake family)

ROOKY

This is our wonderful dog Rooky, which we got from the Home last year. He settled down with us very quickly and is much loved by everybody. Many thanks.

Judith Shirley

DOGS AND HOLIDAYS

As a pet owner one of your important responsibilities is to ensure that your pet will be adequately cared for while you are away from home.

TAKING YOUR DOG WITH YOU

Special travel arrangements will need to be made if your dog is going on holiday with you. Although most dogs enjoy travelling by car, some find this experience rather frightening and may display fear or even dribble or vomit. Training and appropriate medication as advised by a veterinary surgeon should help to reduce these problems. Taking your dog on frequent short journeys in the car should also help him to get used to travelling in this way.

If possible avoid feeding your dog within two hours of starting out and remember to allow time on the journey for stops so your dog can stretch his legs and relieve himself! You should also take drinking water and a bowl.

You should make sure that your dog is restrained in the car so he cannot jump from an open window or distract the driver. A dog guard is a very useful way of keeping a dog in the rear compartment of a car. Never let your dog put his head out of an open window when the car is moving.

Never leave your dog in a closed car in hot sunshine – you may find him dead on your return. If you must leave your dog in the car, park in the shade (allowing for the sun's movement during the day) and leave the windows open a few inches. If you think the sun could shine through any of the windows, cover them with a cloth to reduce the glare and the heat. Remember to leave a bowl of water in the car too and, if possible, return frequently to check that your dog is all right.

If you are travelling by train with your dog make sure you keep your pet with you at all times, otherwise he may suffer the indignity and possible stress of being muzzled and tied up in the guard's van. Make sure that the journey is not too long and that you can arrange for your dog to relieve himself during the journey.

LEAVING YOUR DOG WITH FRIENDS OR NEIGHBOURS

Ensure that the person you are asking to be 'guardian' while you are away knows exactly what is involved and has enough time to put aside for feeding, supervising and exercising your dog.

Leave clear instructions about diet, grooming, exercise and any particular likes or dislikes your dog may have. Make sure the 'guardian' knows who to contact in an emergency and has the name and address of a veterinary surgeon, along with any money which may be needed to pay for treatment.

Remember that your dog will almost certainly be in strange surroundings, he will miss you and has no way of knowing how long you will be away. It is therefore preferable if he already knows the person who will be his temporary guardian – everything possible should be done to reduce his anxiety and uncertainty.

LEAVING YOUR DOG IN KENNELS

Boarding kennels should be booked well in advance to ensure your pet will be staying at the kennel of your choice. It is important that you inspect the kennel for yourself and do not rely simply on the recommendations of others (see page 180).

The dog that begged to live . . . twice

Alfie was very ill and was due to be destroyed. When it was his turn, he just sat up and begged . . . and begged. Nobody had the heart to take the little dog further as he sat waving his paws – and he earned a reprieve. Through the combined efforts of the Battersea staff, Alfie was made well and found a home. However not long afterwards Alfie was back . . . begging once more to the staff. Everybody knew him, and this time nobody had the heart to do anything other than make sure he would be happy until the end of his days. The little 'beggar' had made his point with dignity, and was sent to the country annexe of the Home to end his days quietly

Freddie Reed

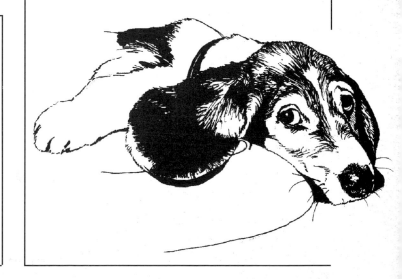

Feeding and Grooming

Feeding times are a highlight in any dog's day. Correct, balanced meals at regular feeding times are of great importance to your puppy and the routine should be strictly observed, especially during the first six months or so. If a puppy has no appetite there is something wrong. Healthy puppies and adult dogs look forward to their feeding times and approach their meals with enthusiasm. It is not unusual for some adult dogs to refuse the occasional meal but if a puppy refuses a meal, there is cause for concern. If meals are refused for more than 24 hours seek veterinary advice. Check, too, that your puppy has not been stuffing itself with something other than its proper diet – anything from cheese to chicken meal, compost or coal.

Never overfeed a dog or puppy. This will lead to obesity which is one of the major contributors to ill-health, particularly in later life.

A typical daily diet for a puppy up to three months old would be as follows:
8.30am: breakfast of milk and wholewheat cereal, such as Weetabix, Shredded Wheat, rusks etc. Alternative: scrambled egg mixed with a little dry cereal.
12.30pm: meat mince mixed with moistened puppy biscuit in equal amounts.
4.30pm: scrambled egg with a little brown bread soaked in milk. Rice pudding is an alternative.
8.30pm: repeat of midday meal.

Minced meat can be beef, chicken, or lamb, but not pork or liver (butcher's pet mince often contains the latter). White fish or green tripe (available from pet shops) can be fed and there are various suitable tinned puppy foods.

The puppy will need food at these regular intervals, every four hours throughout the day, for the first three months. During this time you will discover the puppy's preferences, which will help you decide its later feeding regime.

At the age of three months meals can be reduced to three per day, eliminating one feed slowly by bringing the times of the midday and afternoon meals gradually closer together. You may then be feeding the second meal around mid afternoon. This meal is gradually fed

Clean, fresh water should be available at all times

later in the afternoon until, at four months, the 8.30pm meal is eliminated. Your puppy will then only need two meals, in the early morning and late afternoon.

Around six months, one main meal will replace the two. This is best fed late in the afternoon if possible. You may want to introduce this over some months by gradually reducing the size of the morning meal. Generally, as the dog grows, it will become less interested in earlier meals and focus on the main meal at the end of the day. A small early morning breakfast, however, can be retained and should consist of, for instance, a few dog biscuits and a bowl of milk, or a little scrambled egg if you are cooking some for yourself.

The amount of food required by a dog will depend on weight and activity as well as age. As a guideline, the average non-working but active dog should receive daily, for every 9-11kg (20-25lb) of dog weight, about 110-170g (4-6oz) of meat mixed with approximately 225g(8oz) of biscuit meal plus 30g (1oz) 'extras' such as suitable scraps, egg, cheese, etc.

Between-meals 'titbits' should not be fed to dogs. Most canine appetites allow for consumption of food willingly at any time but this is good for neither health nor temperament. An overfed fat dog becomes unhealthy and unhappy, forced to be lazy and sometimes irritable. Additional weight creates strain on body and internal organs, and makes a dog much less able to fight off illness. The dangers of obesity cannot be underestimated, so always feed just enough to satisfy the dog without overfeeding it. The amount of food provided after six months of age should increase slowly until the dog reaches adulthood, but this must not get out of hand.

Feed as near as possible to the same times each day, and in the same place. Mealtimes should be interesting and exciting events for the dog so that he can enjoy his anticipation of them.

If you have more than one dog in the family, make sure that they are all fed simultaneously. Supervise them to ensure that those who eat more slowly are not pushed aside by the faster eaters.

Long-legged dogs such as Salukis and Afghans need to have their

Making mealtimes fun

It is always worthwhile making feeding times interesting events. Let your dog 'join in' while you are preparing its food – the sights and smell will stimulate digestive juices and appetite. He should be encouraged to sit quietly and watch, rather than to jump around barking noisily. Call your dog when you are about to prepare dinner and try to do it from the same place each day. As the dog learns he will soon remind you when dinner time is approaching, making it fun for both of you.

feeding dishes placed on a low bench so that they do not need to bend their heads down between spread forelegs to reach their food. Such contortions can lead to digestive disorders.

The meal should be fed warm and a little moist for optimum acceptability and ease of digestion, but extremes of temperature should be avoided. Stale food or any that has been exposed to possible contamination by flies, pests, parasites or harmful bacteria

Fussy feeders

Blackie Howson of Buxton, Derbyshire (still going strong and enjoying a good bark at seventeen), loves peas, carrots and eggs but will not touch dog biscuits. Bobby Holt, now seventeen and without a tooth in his head, is also still leaping round like a two-year-old. Another Woolly Whitejaw, he always has cornflakes for breakfast, but only if they are served in a basket in front of the fire. His normal diet consists of chicken breasts or lamb tongues. He tolerates breast of lamb, but reproachfully leaves the fat all round the edge of his bowl. Having been reared on tinned baby-food as a puppy, he refuses to touch anything tinned – even if it's corned beef or stewing steak.

A large dog such as this Great Dane will need her feed bowl raised off the ground. Not so her small companion . . .

should never be used. Dogs should not be fed in direct sunlight in summer – find a shady cool place. Clean, cool, fresh drinking water should be available at all times throughout the day and night.

Observe your dog during the meal to learn about his health. Eager acceptance of food is normal and any reticence to eat may indicate approaching bad health. If he consistently refuses food over two or three days a veterinarian should be consulted.

CHOOSING A DIET

When considering a diet for your dog, remember that food is consumed to provide energy. Anything which the dog's digestive system cannot convert for this purpose is useless and sometimes even harmful. The chosen diet should be balanced and varied and generally based on four principles. Firstly, it should be varied enough over, say, a weekly period to provide the optimum nutritional requirements. Secondly, it must be sufficient to provide the dog with the energy required for its normal weight, lifestyle, and age (but no more). As an extreme example, a large, young working dog will obviously need substantially more food intake than a small, elderly pet.

Thirdly, the balance of the diet, in terms of proteins, fats carbohydrates, vitamins and minerals, should be consistently adequate. Fourthly, and not least in importance, the dog should enjoy it.

Protein is to be found in such foods as meat, eggs, cheese and fish; carbohydrate in biscuit meal, cereals and brown bread, and fats in meat fat, fish oils and milk. Some dogs are unable to tolerate cow's milk, an intolerance symptomised by bouts of diarrhoea. They may well be able to take goat's milk, however, if some is available.

Proteins help with the growth and repair of body tissue and contribute to the production of energy. Fats are highly efficient energy producers and also repair fat wastage. They provide about twice the energy per unit weight of proteins and carbohydrates. They add palatability to food and can often be used to encourage a reluctant dog to eat. Carbohydrates also provide energy and can be converted to body fat. They are, however, of less value to the dog's metabolism than fats or proteins.

Meat should be free from bones, particularly those of the small, spiky variety which are frequently lethal. It can be varied to include beef, lamb, rabbit, chicken, (kidney and liver for adult dogs only), tripe, heart, ox-cheek etc.

A diet of meat alone is to be avoided as it lacks calcium and phosphorus, both of which are necessary for healthy growth. Bone meal is a useful source of both of these minerals, but use only that which is prepared especially for canine consumption. Meat should always be cooked, primarily to kill any harmful bacteria which may be present, and mixed with a good quality biscuit meal. Bone-free fish is often enjoyed by dogs and is a valuable dietary alternative to meat on occasions.

Minerals such as calcium and phosphorus are present in the dog in larger amounts than trace elements such as iron, zinc, selenium and iodine. There is a close relationship and vital balance to be maintained between calcium and phosphorus which are linked to vitamin D requirements. Calcium is also necessary for several stages of the blood clotting process and for nerve and muscle activity. A deficiency can lead to spasms and paralysis as well as to bone disorders. The correct calcium/phosphorus balance is doubly important to the whelping bitch: if the balance is tipped in favour of phosphorus, bone formation and repair is affected, but high calcium can be harmful.

Rules of the Garden

The garden need not be a problem if you regard it as just another 'rule of life' which your dog has to learn. With your puppy on the lead, walk around those parts of the garden where it is allowed to go. Bitch urine burns the grass, so if you are lawn-proud, throw a bucket of water on the urine to dilute it. If the lawn is not taboo, and it's not raining, stand out there together for a while having a peaceful think. Do this for several days, so that the puppy comes to realise where it is allowed to walk. Then, one day when the edge has been taken off his energy, remove the lead. If he wanders away from you but only where he is allowed, call him to you and praise him. If he heads for the nearest flower bed, just as he reaches it, say 'NO' and put him back where he should be. Within a few days he should come to understand your Rules of the Garden.

Phosphorus also features in various energy conversion processes.

Sodium chloride (salt) is absorbed in minute quantities in a dog's diet, together with potassium which is in many foodstuffs. Sodium is needed for healthy cell growth while potassium is needed for fluid balance, nerve impulse transmission and effective muscle operation.

Other important nutritional 'ingredients' which are generally present in a varied diet include magnesium, copper, zinc and selenium as well as iodine, cobalt and manganese. There are also fourteen main vitamins which are essential for the dog's health and growth and which are found in a good balanced diet. By providing your dog with such a diet, deficiencies will normally be prevented. If they should occur – or be caused by disease – specific symptoms will generally reflect these deficiencies and a veterinarian will act to correct the levels by supplements. An excess of some minerals or vitamins may produce a toxic effect and a careful monitoring is needed by the veterinarian to ensure that the correct balance is attained and not exceeded.

There are some very good proprietary brands of canned dog food available (and also some nutritionally poor ones usually costing less

Faithful friend, ally and support

and with a low meat and high cereal content). The better brands, when mixed with a good proprietary biscuit meal soaked in gravy or warm water, offer a balanced diet and your dog will generally make its own choice. The better brands of biscuit meal also contain such minerals as calcium, phosphorus and magnesium with vitamins, fats, oils and cereals. Contents are usually listed on the packet and this factor is perhaps the best reason for buying branded, as opposed to loose, unlabelled pet-shop-type biscuit. Brown bread is an acceptable alternative to biscuit meal.

Liver is a good supplementary source of vitamins A and D (as well as proteins and fats). These important vitamins are also found in cod-liver and halibut-liver oils. Do not feed liver, or foods containing liver, more than once or twice a week irregularly (and never to young puppies) or the recipient may respond with an attack of diarrhoea.

The only bones to be fed to a dog should be large beef marrow bones or clean ribs. They have virtually no dietary use but are helpful for teeth cleaning and entertainment for the dog. Marrow can, of course, be extracted from the bone after the dog has chewed it (if you can get to it before it is buried in the flower bed). Merely dip the handle of a spoon or meat skewer into it and feed it directly to the dog. It will be much enjoyed and provides extra fat and protein.

Eggs are useful, being rich in proteins, vitamins (including A, D and B^{12}), iron and other nutrients. Raw eggs can be added occasionally to the dog's dinner but they are better cooked, since raw egg whites may be difficult for the dog to digest and they contain a substance altered by cooking which prevents the absorption of a useful vitamin.

Some cooked vegetables are enjoyed by dogs; eg peas and beans (French, broad and runner), which are fairly rich in protein and B vitamins. Cabbage, lettuce, cauliflower and Brussels sprouts are of little nutritional value to the dog. Potatoes cannot be digested raw and should never be fed in this form, though small amounts of cooked potatoes may be acceptable. Cooked carrots provide some vitamin A if fresh. These vegetables and cooked rice can be included in the diet in small quantities only (probably as household scraps) for their bulk/ fibre value, though they contain little nutritional value to the dog. Some vegetables may cause indigestion to individual dogs.

Specially formulated dry 'complete' foods are now widely available. They are often cereal based with added nutrients. These are a complete meal in themselves and should not be confused with dry biscuit 'mixer' meal mentioned above.Complete dry dog foods are more convenient to feed and store and can be very successful, but they are not popular with every dog. Some dogs need the added interest of a more varied diet. You will soon be able to tell if your dog is happy with a complete food.

Water forms a vital part of all dogs' diets and should always be available. A dog's metabolism and health are drastically affected if denied water. A working dog, for example, will be 50 per cent less efficient if it cannot reach water.

Special diets are sometimes needed for sick, elderly, post-operative and whelping animals (see page 160).

GROOMING

Regular grooming is essential to good health. It should begin in puppyhood so that your dog becomes used to the brush and comb and enjoys the session.

Grooming should include attention to ears , eyes, teeth, mouth and feet. It is a good opportunity to check your dog over; to feel for any lumps or bumps, external parasites, damage or disease. It keeps the dog alert, clean and, very importantly, makes him feel good.

Bitches need regular careful examination around the mammary glands and abdomen for any sign of growth. Both sexes can be inspected during grooming for anal gland problems or inflammation.

Short-haired dogs need less brushing (and even less combing) than long-haired breeds, but all need some brushing to prevent dandruff, discourage external parasites, clean the coat and clear tangles. A grooming session once a week is usually sufficient for all but the very long-haired breeds, such as Afghan hounds, Pekinese, Shi Tzu, etc, which need daily attention.

Nobody ever asks my opinion . . .

. . . and mind my eye!

But it was all worth it in the end

Grooming equipment for a short-haired dog should include brush, dental scaler, a chamois leather (or piece of velvet) and a dog's nail file for tidying claws. For long-haired dogs you will require in addition one or more steel combs with varying distances between the teeth, a tangle-comb, mat splitter (for combing and cutting tangles and matted fur), toe scissors (for clipping hair between the claws and pads) and suitable round-tipped scissors (not sharp-pointed ones which are responsible for many grooming accidents). A stainless-steel bowl is also useful for washing round eyes and other orifices, where necessary (with cotton wool).

Bristle brushes are preferable to the wire variety, and the choice of steel comb will depend largely on the type and thickness of the coat (avoiding painful tugging). A dental scaler is needed to remove any accumulation of tartar on the teeth, particularly in older dogs. Any difficulty with this operation should be referred to a veterinarian to prevent scraping the enamel of the teeth or other dental damage. The chamois leather or velvet cloth adds a fine shine to the dog's coat after brushing.

A great deal of time and expertise is needed to achieve a result like this perfectly groomed American Cocker Spaniel

A tangle comb is shaped rather like a miniature short-handled garden rake and is best used in conjunction with a mat splitter (a hand-sized, scythe-shaped instrument with a blade at one end) to cut and disentangle the most obstinate of mats in the fur. Beware of the sharp blade on the splitter and do not poke it into the dog's skin.

A variety of electric hand clippers is available, should it be necessary to strip a dog during hot weather. Follow the manufacturer's instructions carefully and/or buy a book on the subject. Most students of this craft learn best by trial and error, so it is advisable to buy clippers with adjustable blades. Begin by taking off only a little fur on the fine adjustment and adapt as you become more confident (and successful).

Groom your dog, if possible, on a firm non-slippery bench or table with a surface that is conveniently level with your chest. Talk to your dog while it is being groomed and make it a happy event for both of you. Talking will sooth the dog if it is apprehensive and the task will become easier when he looks forward to the sessions as an enjoyable experience.

Regular bathing is really only necessary when the dog's coat becomes contaminated, smelly or dirty, perhaps through rolling in some foul-smelling substance. Eucalyptus oil will remove any oily contaminant – rub it into the affected area before washing. Regular grooming generally removes the need for bathing under normal circumstances. Show dogs are bathed before a show, but two or three

EMMA AND KATE

Mother gave me Emma one May evening. It was, I remember, a typically Cornish May evening, with a clear, soft blue sky, still warm after a perfect early summer day. Ever since meeting my first Golden Retriever some twenty years before, I had always admired their beauty, high intelligence and that super-soft gundog temperament.

Our beloved Dalmatian bitch, Dita, had just died so the enormous hole had to be filled with a puppy. She was a warm, furry, cuddly teddy-bear, with a pale golden coat, very dark ears, jet black nose and the sweetest, most irresistible face. She was such a friendly little soul – definitely the pup of my dreams. So, having been shown the pedigree (which meant very little to me then but later proved to be all I could want of Golden bloodlines) and been approved by Emma's 'mum' and the breeder, a cheque changed hands and the pup was mine.

I named her Emma during the journey home and later registered her as Demerara Daydream because she sat for hours staring into space, daydreaming in

the sun. She was also the colour of demerara sugar – and every bit as sweet!

Emma was a model puppy. Typical of her breed, she was eager, kind, with a great desire to please. She settled in immediately, never made a sound at night and was already 'self' house-trained. Little did I then realise that puppies do house-train themselves, given the opportunity. The days were long and sunny, and she spent most of her time playing in the garden while being admired by passers-by. There would often be a group of people leaning on our wall, talking to Emma. She expected everyone to make a fuss of her. She adores men, and will go out of her way to find and flirt with one. She seemed, too, to be a thought-reader. I never had to teach her anything, and she passed on her knowledge to her children, grand-children and especially her great-grandson, Cinnamon – *the* most intelligent dog I've ever known. When I was in the garden he had two different barks to tell me if the doorbell or telephone were ringing. And many times people told me that he had 'answered' the phone

baths a year should be enough for other dogs.

When bathing your dog, use a good dog shampoo, never a human one, to preserve the natural oils of the dog's coat. An insecticidal shampoo should help to eliminate and prevent external parasites.

Stand the dog in the bath, on a rubber mat to prevent it being frightened by its feet slipping. Dogs are particularly frightened of slippery surfaces which will make them very wary of future baths (or other handling). Have two non-fluffy towels ready close at hand so that you do not need to leave your dog to fetch one. Rinse the coat first with warm water – a shower is useful. Then rub in the dog shampoo to a fine lather, keeping it well away from the eyes and the insides of the ears. Rinse again with more warm water until all traces of shampoo have vanished. Dry the dog thoroughly, paying special attention to the creases around thighs and 'armpits', between toes, under the tail and around the genital area. Use the second towel to dry the head, eyes and ears. Be gentle and thorough. Ideally, finish the operation with a clean, soft chamois leather. Some dogs enjoy the warm air from a hair dryer, but keep it away from the eyes, insides of ears and under the tail in particular.

A dog may be bathed before a meal but not for three hours after, and should not be bathed outside in cold weather. Never bath a bitch in season or close to whelping, nor a sick or recuperating dog. Extra care and special gentleness are needed when bathing (or grooming) an aged dog.

Grooming time

When you are choosing a dog, consider the amount of care the adult coat may need. With smooth-coated dogs, such as pointers, Great Danes and Dalmatians, grooming isn't too much of a problem; but if you decide on an Afghan or an Old English Sheepdog you will probably have to spend time each day combing out knots and tangles. An Old English Sheepdog called Hobson is groomed for about half-an-hour daily, using a brush and two metal combs of different sizes – the finer-toothed comb for teasing out knots on paws, legs, head, beard and ears and the coarser comb for back and sides. Hobson was also trained when young to lie on his back while his sides, belly and inside-legs are brushed and/or gently combed.

when I was out.

Then I decided to have a second dog, and there was a litter of English Setters for sale in Devon. The eight lovely puppies, almost eight weeks old, were a very even litter being closely line-bred to the top show winner and stud dog. They bounced about so much that it was impossible to count them let alone distinguish one from another. They played dreadfully rough games, dragging one another about by the ears and shrieking with delight, especially at the sight of a great bowl of milky food. They plastered milk all over their faces and over their heads and backs so that the breeder had to dry them all before they could continue their wrestling matches. Then 'mum' arrived to see that her babies were all right. She was absolutely gorgeous; a pretty, elegant, light tri.

I bought a dark tri bitch with a black ear and a wicked expression, and that marked the end of the peaceful summer with gentle Emma. Life with a setter is full of surprises and can never be dull. Kate (from *The Taming of the Shrew*) had entered our lives and was determined to make her presence felt. Whereas Emma's first night in her new home had been peaceful and puddle-free, Kate's first night was hell. She was put to bed in a very convenient corner of the kitchen, under a worktop, with cupboards on either side to keep her cosy and draught free, plus a board and heavy table across the corner to make her feel secure. A new cardboard box, lots of blankets, a metal hot-water bottle well wrapped in an old sweater, and plenty of newspapers on the floor, made a lovely nursery for the new baby. Or so I thought!

At some unearthly hour in the night we were awakened by Kate's cries. We left her at first to get on with it, not wanting her to associate howling with the way to attract attention. Eventually, however, I went to comfort the puppy. Emma, of course, had a smug look on her face – she never made a noise like that. And there was Kate, with puddles all over the place. A change of bedding, clean newspaper, renewed hot-water bottle, quick cuddle and lights out. Kate was soon howling her head off again. More puddles to clear up. I gave her a rusk, which went in a flash. So I left her with a large, hard dog biscuit to suck. Not another sound was heard until daybreak, when I came downstairs. Imagine my surprise upon entering the kitchen to find that Kate had not only eaten the very large, very hard dog biscuit but had also moved the heavy wooden table, and the board, and was sitting by the door, waiting for us.

Heroic Dogs

In 1978 the PRO-Dogs national charity decided to arrange an annual awards ceremony to honour brave and devoted dogs. Three categories were designated: Life Saving, Devotion to Duty and Pet of the Year. These were to cover dogs involved in saving human life or in police service, and other dogs acting courageously beyond the normal call of duty, plus family or famous dogs helping in some unusual way. The first year involved intensive research seeking brave dogs, but three outstandingly deserving dogs received the first medals on 9 December 1979. Ever since, nominations have been pouring in. The majority of medals have been presented to dogs which have already made headlines in the national or local press.

The first medal for Devotion to Duty was presented to Rats, who served with the army in Northern Ireland and has since become something of a legend in his own lifetime (see page 150).

SANDY

In the same year, the medal for Life Saving was presented to a strong yellow Labrador/Retriever called Sandy. Two seventeen-year-old youths went for a swim in the Thames at Egham, Surrey, but neither was aware of the treacherous corkscrew currents in that part of the river. Gary Dodd got into difficulties whilst trying to reach mooring posts and he was sucked under four times. His friend Darren Conner went to his rescue and helped to keep him afloat, but soon got into difficulties himself.

At this point, Mr Osmond Sambrook was walking along the river bank with his ten-year-old dog Sandy and heard their cries for help. Mr Sambrook dived in and dragged Gary to safety, but by this time Darren was exhausted and started struggling desperately. Then Sandy joined in the rescue. He jumped into the river and circled the lad several times, almost as if he was inviting Darren to hold on to him. Darren grabbed Sandy round the neck, and, despite the considerable weight, the dog eventually pulled Darren to the safety of the bank.

Mr Sambrook played down his own brave part in the rescue but said of Sandy, 'It was his retriever instincts coming out. Sandy is enormously strong and an extraordinary dog. Darren would certainly

---

Dogs in cars

It is important to train your dog not to jump out of the car immediately after the door is opened. This is one of the areas where the 'Wait' command is very important.

have drowned without his help. . . I am astonished at what he did, because he always stays very close by my side. On this occasion he acted on his own initiative in answer to the cries for help and swam about 40ft out into the river to help Darren.'

GOLDIE AND SCHNORBITZ

Well known dogs often receive nominations for PRO Dog's Pet of the Year medal, particularly from children. Goldie the Golden Retriever from the BBC television programme *Blue Peter* received this medal in 1981. She was nominated by nine year old Jessica McConnell who was unable to have a dog at home herself. She wrote that she felt Goldie should receive a medal 'for all the children who have not got a dog, because she is our dog to share'.

In 1986, Bernie Winter's famous St Bernard, Schnorbitz, received the Pet of the Year medal by popular demand. Bernie and Schnorbitz are certainly great company and with a continual stream of wise cracks for the national press, always assembled on these occasions, Bernie made the whole party go with a swing.

KALLI

Kalli lived at Guilsborough Grange bird and pet park in Northamptonshire and was a gentle natured cross-bred collie bitch. Many orphan baby animals found their way to the park and Kalli was willing to mother them all. By the age of four years, when she received her gold medal award, she had suckled, cleaned and helped to rear two Arctic fox cubs, two pumas, one lion and one tiger cub.

Fireworks

Despite numerous warnings to owners, many pets, including dogs, are burned, injured and frightened each year by fireworks and bonfires. The method of prevention is simple: keep all dogs inside the house behind closed curtains when fireworks are being used. If, in an emergency, a dog must go outside, it must be accompanied and on a lead, and be brought inside again as soon as possible.

Surrogate mother Kalli with the tiger cub she helped to rear at Guilsborough Grange Wildlife Park, Northamptonshire

Even when these orphans were fully grown they treated their 'mother' with great respect, though they could probably have knocked her senseless with a single blow from a powerful paw.

NIPPER

Nipper won an award in 1985. He defeated the strong instinctive fear of smoke and fire which all animals have in order to bring a flock of 300 ewes and lambs out of a burning barn. The bleating of the terrified animals had quickly brought farm workers to the scene but the smoke was already so acrid and thick they had to give up hope of rescuing the sheep.

But Nipper, with paws burnt and lungs filled with smoke, braved the conditions and brought nearly all the flock to safety. He worked without commands as best he could, with the sound of the terrified animals to spur him on. Some of the very young lambs would not be moved, and this drove the frantic mothers back after they had been taken to safety, to seek out their bleating lambs. Nipper returned again and again, until finally all were out of the barn. Nearly all survived.

The citation for Nipper's medal for Devotion to Duty reads, 'For bravery in overcoming the danger and fear of fire to rescue his sheep'.

Opposite:
Nipper, the brave farm dog, who rescued 300 sheep from a burning barn

Power and vitality in full flight

MAX

Max, a medium-sized 'rescued' mongrel terrier won the medal for Life Saving (1988), with the citation, 'For bravely stopping the kidnapping of a child'.

Max's mother was discovered when she was about to give birth in a nest in a hayfield. The villagers of Kippax, near Leeds, took pity on the bitch and found a home for her and all seven of the pups. Max went to the family of Joseph and Judith Harrison, Michelle and eleven-year-old Vicky – although Mrs Harrison was not at all keen on having a dog.

One evening, Vicky called out to the family that she was taking Max for a walk, and was out of the door before anyone could stop her. With Max on his lead they set off down the well lit High Street and then turned off into a quiet street near a school. Vicky became alarmed when a car drew up and the door opened. A man wearing a balaclava jumped out and she could see that the driver also wore a balaclava. She was told to get into the car, but refused, whereupon the man grabbed her, putting his hand over her mouth to keep her quiet.

Max promptly sank his teeth into the man's leg. When the man hit Vicky, Max went for his hand, giving Vicky a moment to escape. She dodged away, running through a cutting where it was impossible for a car to follow. Vicky reached home safely and the police were called at once. Max reached home shortly afterwards, covered in blood and, it was feared, badly hurt. However, it turned out that nearly all the blood was from Vicky's would-be captor and this was helpful to the police. Vicky herself is in no doubt about how much she owed to Max. 'He saved my life,' she says.

SAMMY

The award for Devotion to Duty 1988 went to a German Shepherd called Sammy, with the citation, 'For bravery in protecting his owner from a rogue horse'.

Whilst Bernadette Barton was out walking her dogs in Smallfield, Surrey, a stallion which had been turned out by gypsies suddenly raced towards them. Sammy knows horses well and exercises daily with them and his horse-riding owner. He sensed that Bernadette was in danger and, despite her command to the dogs to return to the car for safety, Sammy stayed with Bernadette, placing himself between her and the rearing stallion. As the horse crashed down on the head

---

Snake-bite

Death from snake-bite is rare in the UK since the only venomous snake likely to be encountered by a dog on a walk in the countryside is the adder or viper. While the adder varies in description between individuals there is little difficulty in distinguishing it from the other two British snakes. The adder has a dark zig-zag stripe down the middle of its back and there is usually an inverted V or X-shaped mark on the head. The iris of the eye is copper-coloured. It is found in many types of countryside throughout the British Isles, though it shows a preference for open places where sun is plentiful; on sandy heaths, moorland, hillsides, open sunny places in woodland and rough common land, for example. In the spring, groups of them, recently emerged from hibernation, may be seen together.

of the dog, Sammy screamed in pain and collapsed on the ground, but Bernadette was safe and the horse trotted off. Sammy suffered serious injuries, losing his right eye, but he continues his obedience work and even competes in agility competitions.

JAMES

Pet of the Year 1988 went to a tri-colour Corgi called James, with the citation, 'For being a dog of Royal breeding, working as a PAT dog'.

James was born in Windsor Castle to be exact, and his breeder is the world's most famous Corgi owner, HM Queen Elizabeth II. As the Queen keeps only bitches from the litters that she breeds, dogs are sometimes given to good homes. James was lucky at the age of four months to go to Daphne Slark who was for many years with the well known Rozavel kennels of Mrs Thelma Gray, who supplied the Royal Family's first Corgis back in the thirties.

His noble birth has not prevented James from being a wonderful pet – or from tackling a job of work as a registered PAT dog, visiting the residents of a nursing home near Haverfordwest.

JET, LOCK AND MEG

Three remarkable search and rescue dogs have also won gold medals. The first was Jet who won the Devotion to Duty medal in 1983, with the citation, 'For Courage and persistence in mountain rescue'.

Moments of triumph come seldom for individual members of hard-working mountain rescue teams, but the outstanding man-and-dog partnership of Phillip Benbow and Jet saved lost people in Snowdonia on three occasions in one year.

They saved twelve-year-old Julian Smith and his eleven-year-old sister Catherine in October 1982. An RAF helicopter had been beaten back by the gale, but the mountain rescue dogs and their volunteer handlers set off in near freezing conditions to search, until a break was called at 3.00am. Phillip Benbow offered to continue the search with Jet, and the extra effort was rewarded soon after 4.00am when the two children were found by the searching dog. Both children were safe, but cold and frightened by their twenty-hour ordeal in a crevice at 2,000ft.

Mr Benbow said, 'Although we often train, Jet knows well enough when it's for real – and then he is excited and works with great determination, tirelessly.'

Proud possessions

Mr C. Hughes, a country comedian, had a wig which generally hung on a peg in one of his rooms. He one day lent the wig to a brother player, and some time afterwards called on him. Mr Hughes had his Dog with him, and the man happened to have the borrowed wig on his head. Mr Hughes stayed a little while with his friend; but, when he left him, the Dog remained behind. For some time he stood, looking full in the man's face; then, making a sudden spring, he leaped on his shoulders, seized the wig, and ran off with it as fast as he could; and when he reached home, he endeavoured, by jumping, to hang it up in its usual place. The same Dog was one afternoon passing through a field near Dartmouth, where a washer-woman had hung out her linen to dry. He stopped and surveyed one particular shirt with attention; then seizing it, he dragged it away through the dirt to his master, whose shirt it proved to be.

Nineteenth-century anecdote

*Three courageous dogs; (centre)
Jacob, who rescued his owner's
handbag from a mugger, with
Meg and Lock who helped to save
life in the aftermath of the
El Salvador earthquake disaster*

PRO-Dogs

PRO-Dogs is always pleased to
receive any press cuttings about
brave and special dogs, and
nominations to consider for the
annual gold medal awards. If
your dog deserves a medal, write
to Lesley Scott-Ordish at PRO-
Dogs (see Useful Addresses).

It is as if the dogs pick up and understand the urgent need to find,
working with all the other dogs as members of the team, systematically
covering large areas of ground together, far greater in range than men
could achieve. The super-scenting ability of the dog, together with
the ready eagerness to please, means that man and dog together
succeed, where man alone would fail. The dog picks up air-borne
scent and therefore has an ability to detect quite outside the experience
of people.

These same skills were used by British dogs sent out to help find

people and bodies following the earthquake disaster in El Salvador in October 1986. (Dogs from other countries were used to good effect in the more recent dreadful earthquake disaster in Armenia in December 1988). Lock and Meg, working collies owned by Mr Dave Riley and Mr Davy Jones, received their gold medals from PRO Dogs in 1987. On their return from El Salvador Lock and Meg had to undergo the obligatory six months in quarantine, but they were given the treatment which heroes deserve as far as was possible, and were soon back at work with the search and rescue dog team.

Training the Young Dog

GENERAL PRINCIPLES

An unruly dog is, at best, often a nuisance to the community in which he lives and, at worst, can become a positive danger. On the other hand, a well-behaved, obedient dog is a pleasure to own, and because he regards himself as a member of a pack of which his owner is leader, he expects to be treated accordingly and is far happier than the totally undisciplined dog, who is probably made miserable by constant chastisement and nagging.

It is therefore the moral and legal responsibility of all dog owners to ensure that their charges are trained to a socially acceptable standard – and the larger the dog the more important this becomes.

The basic requirements for achieving this end are simply to train the dog to come when called, walk to heel on and off the lead, and to sit, lie down, and stay on command. Once these exercises have become thoroughly established then the owner, if sufficiently enthusiastic and if the dog's temperament is suitable, may progress to more advanced work. The aim of this article, however, is merely to point the way to turning a young dog into a pleasing, responsive and happy companion that its owner will be proud to take anywhere.

All dogs – pedigree and mongrel alike – can be successfully trained, at least in the basics, although some are more receptive than others and therefore learn quicker. Such receptivity is not, however, necessarily indicative of a higher intelligence, in fact many highly intelligent dogs require longer to train because they are inclined to be more independent and in the wild state would probably become pack leaders.

The training described here is generally begun at any age from about eight or nine months to two years, depending upon the dogs' level of maturity. Some few may be started a little earlier than eight months, but in most cases it is best to wait at least until that age. Dogs over two years are by no means beyond training, although the older they are the longer they may take to learn new exercises.

Although there are establishments to which dogs may be sent for training, it is preferable, for both the dog and the owner, to train together from the beginning as the bond of attachment between them will be strengthened through their developing understanding of each

---

You are the pack leader

The dog is a pack animal, even though it may be the only one living with you. If you have several dogs, they each know their 'pecking' order so do not try to equalise it. You are pack leader, the boss. It is most important to establish this, particularly if you have only one dog. A dog respects the pack leader and looks to him or her for food, comfort and instruction. Without this respect and guidance a dog may become 'difficult' because it doesn't know where it fits in and, therefore, feels completely lost.

Opposite:
You're never too young to learn – or to teach

106

other. Moreover, a dog works far better with someone he knows and trusts and whom he regards as his 'leader'.

Reputable dog-training clubs are much better and, in fact, are strongly recommended. There the owners and dogs are taught together and the owner/handler will assist in preventing the formation of bad habits and will be available to give advice on individual problems.

HEEL WORK ON THE LEAD

By the time a puppy reaches the age of 8 or 9 months he should be responding well when called by name, walking freely on the lead, and should leave whatever he is doing – or about to do – when he

THE CHALLENGE

I watched the two puppies through a mist of tears. It all seemed so unfair. There they lay, so beautiful and so crippled.

This was a much-wanted litter, carefully planned, carefully reared. Only as the days went by did it become obvious that something was wrong. All had been a bit slow, but these, the absolute best, were totally handicapped.

I observed them. One had given up. He lay on his belly, legs out like a starfish: I picked him up, and he cried out. Underneath, he was red raw where he had lain flat for eight weeks, growing heavier all the time, unable to move. I tried to manipulate his joints. It was hopeless. Gently, I put him back. He was so beautiful. How could nature be so cruel?

The other pup was trying to rise, trying, and trying again, his useless little legs collapsing beneath him, yet again he would try. I lifted him, and at once he arched his spine, his legs coming up for all the world like weird chicken's wings, but at least he could move. I worked his limbs back into their sockets. They could be manipulated, apparently without pain, even though they slipped out again. I put him down. At once he tried to rise. What a gutsy little boy! Surely he deserved a chance?

'I don't think there's any hope for that one', I said, indicating the other sad little soul, ' but would you let me take this one and see what I can do?' The breeder was only too pleased. She knew she had not the time, nor the will, but hoped I had. We wrapped the strange little body in a blanket, and put him into a box to take home.

Thus began the most frustrating, exciting, miserable, and yet rewarding time of my life. Many people stated that I was crazy. Others remarked that they didn't believe it could be done. Even more said 'Why bother with one like that? You could be making a bit in stud fees while you're feeding him.'

Of course, they were correct. Would anyone in their right mind take on such a cripple? Probably not! We called him Challenge, and he was that all right, but his disability was matched by his determination, and his determination brought out all my own. Somehow we were going to succeed.

THERAPY

It was a beautiful summer that year, day after day of sunshine, and we would go onto the lawn for therapy, six times a day, just for a few minutes. Initially, it was mostly a case of massage, manipulating his limbs into place, and holding them there. Then I would sit down, making a passage with my legs, set him in a standing position between my ankles, and encourage him to come towards me. With my legs holding his useless limbs upright, he would try, and soon could take one or two steps. What a brave, determined little scrap he was. Yet sometimes, as he tried to command his limbs and they refused, he would get into such a state of fury and frustration that he would cry out and bite my hands and arms. Then I would pick him up, and we would take a walk round the garden. The apples were beginning to set in the orchard, and he would reach up and try to take them in his mouth. Such a merry little boy, he would soon be his sunny self, and we would try just once more before going indoors.

Being so disabled, Challie would get very sore underneath, so needed to be dusted regularly with talcum powder. There he would lie on his back, like a baby, his lovely eyes beaming up at me, sometimes holding out his hand, but always, whatever problems we had experienced during exercise, loving and happy.

The days went by. It was all a matter of trial and error. Nobody appeared to have tried, or succeeded, with a young puppy as crippled as this. We borrowed a 'baby bouncer' and made a similar device, so that he could keep trying to reach the floor with his feet, but

Dog-training clubs are to be recommended – and they're good fun, too

without weight on his legs. Most of the time it was my hands which did the work, though. With me, he would try and try again. If it was rewarding to see slight improvement, it was also depressing, as often we would seem to slip back to the beginning. His legs *would not* support him, and we were back to holding him up between my legs. Yet gradually he did begin to stand, and then to take a few steps.

Once he was beginning to use his front legs, I made a sling, and we would walk about, he using his front almost normally while his hindlegs just made movement, without weight. This mode of transport he loved, and setting off at the top of the garden we would run down, as in a wheelbarrow race, faster and faster, until we both collapsed on the grass in a breathless heap. Challie's eyes would laugh up at me. 'Come on,' he said, as plainly as speaking, 'Let's do it again!'

Triumph and despair — they filled my days in equal measure. Many times I thought I would have to give up, but how could I, when his courage was so great? Little, beautiful, determined, he would never be quite right, but if only we could get him fairly normal! I had to keep trying.

SPASTIC

Peter was spastic, and worked on the dustbin round, where his disjointed body was a source of amusement to his mates, who delighted in teasing the lad. But because of his own disabilities, Peter comprehended Challie's, and in those early days his encouragement was a blessing. If we were outside when he came, he would limp up the steps to put his hand gently on the little dog's head. 'He's much better this week,' he would say, and if we were indoors he would knock to enquire. In his own way, he helped. If Peter, so disabled, could actually work, surely I could make Challie walk!

One day, with Challie up on the lawn in the sun and I in the kitchen, I looked up and there he was, actually standing up looking in at me, head on one side. I couldn't believe it! He had got up on his own! Almost immediately he fell over, but he had done it! I went out and picked him up, and we waltzed round the garden, I singing, he grinning as widely as I.

Then came the day when he not only stood on his own, but actually set off and walked. The tall blue campanulas were in full bloom, and he staggered towards one, reached up, and caught one of the bright blue bells in his mouth. Turning round to me in triumph, he fell over, but he'd done it, and he knew he'd done it. That was a red-letter day indeed!

So our little successes and failures came as the days went by into autumn. No longer could we have our times outside, and it seemed a big setback when we had to get used to less grip on the floor. I think we both knew it could be done, though. We were not going to be beaten now! He could get up alone and could walk, his back legs were becoming stronger, and he was the happiest little person, playing with the other dogs, falling over, picking himself up and, in his persistent way, starting again.

On Christmas morning we had friends in for drinks, the dogs all around us, my neighbour sitting on a low chair with Challie on the floor beside her. Suddenly he reached up, placed his front paws on her knee, and stood up tall.

Have you ever heard the bells of Heaven ring? They did that morning for me, the loudest, most joyful Christmas peals, for he had overcome the final hurdle. He could stand up on his hindlegs. The little helpless, crippled baby, had become this beautiful person.

Of course, Challie was never quite right, but he remained with us until, at thirteen years of age, he left us to run through the Elysian Fields with many who had gone before him.

All the money we could have made through stud fees would have gone years ago. The joy he brought us through all his brave, merry life, can never be forgotten.

Opposite:
*Sitting to heel – invaluable
while waiting for the opportunity
to cross*

*Heel work on the lead is useful on
busy city pavements*

hears the word 'No' spoken in a firm, slightly reproving tone. His first serious training exercise, for which he is now ready, will be walking to heel on the lead.

For all but the smallest breeds, the first training requirement is a fairly long lead and a check chain (sometimes unfortunately called a 'choke' chain). It is most important to fit the chain so that the running part of the chain – the end to which the lead is attached – passes over the back of the dog's neck. If fitted the other way round, with the running part beneath the neck, it will lock when the lead is pulled and will not slacken off when pressure on the lead is released.

In this exercise the dog is taught to walk close to the left side, keeping his shoulder level with the trainer's knee and without any tendency to get ahead, lag behind, or move outwards away from the trainer's leg. To commence the exercise, position the dog on your left, place the check chain over his head as illustrated and hold the lead in you right hand, which should be about waist high and in the centre of your body.

Start to walk forward, jerking the lead slightly, and give the

Beds and bedding

Unless a dog is to be kept permanently outside where it may sleep in a kennel or barn (for example, in the case of a gundog or farm dog), it should always have its own bed in the house. It can retreat to it in safety when it wishes and rest on it at night. In outside kennels a bed can still be made up with blankets or other soft material as in the house; or soft oat-straw, removed and burnt each week, can be used. If making a bed with old clothing, remove all buttons and fastenings. A lining of clean newspaper acts as a useful insulator during the winter if needed. Never use wood shavings and sawdust as bedding material; the latter is often harmful to respiration and both can be poisonous to the dog. Some woods are themselves poisonous and others used as timber are often treated with a poisonous fungicide. In kennels, wooden beds are often provided. Whatever the bed, it must be raised off the floor to avoid draughts.

One of the best forms of dog bed is the basket. It is usually circular with a small cut-out

continued

command 'heel' in an authoritative voice, pronouncing the work clearly. Take short, crisp steps, not long strides, and it is important to vary the pace from fast to slow, to make the dog concentrate on your movements. Your left hand is employed in encouraging the dog to keep close to you by tapping your side or the top of your thigh.

Do not walk in a long, straight line, but make a number of turns to the left and right and completely turn about frequently, keeping the lead slack and giving the command 'heel' on each change of direction.

Whenever the dog moves away from you, gets ahead or behind, give the lead a sharp jerk with the left hand to bring him back into position, giving the command 'heel' at the same time; never pull or drag the dog along – a sharp jerk is all that is needed. But immediately the dog has regained the correct position, praise him and allow the lead to become slack.

If the dog pulls ahead, jerk the lead upwards and backwards, but never *across* the body, and if he lags behind encourage him with your left hand and your voice. When the dog is maintaining the correct

A young pup has learnt his heel-free exercise well

position be lavish with your praise and he will soon realise that he is pleasing you by keeping close.

As training progresses the jerks on the lead should become less frequent and less vigorous until, finally, there will be no need for correction. At this stage the lead should always be held so lightly in the right hand that the dog is scarcely aware of its presence.

Dogs quickly become bored and daily training exercises should be practised only so long as the dog continues to show interest: when interest begins to waver, take the first opportunity to end for a rest, choosing a moment when everything is going well and praising the dog enthusiastically.

SITTING AT HEEL

When good progress is being made in the heel-on-the-lead exercise, the sit-at-heel can be introduced. As you come briskly to a halt with both feet together, jerk the lead upwards above the dog's head and at the same time push him into the sit position by exerting pressure over the loins with the left hand, accompanied by the command 'SIT', uttering the word explosively with the emphasis on the 'T'. If the sitting position is not perfectly aligned with your leg, bend your knees and place the dog accurately but do not repeat the command – repeated commands lose their impact and teach the dog to wait to be told several times before obeying.

Once this exercise has been well learned, the dog will sit in response to the slight upward jerk on the lead without the command, and soon he should sit automatically when you halt, without command or signal.

Remember to be firm and persistent and never let your dog get away with a slovenly performance – but equally essential are patience and kindness with plenty of praise for an exercise well done.

HEEL-FREE

When the dog is fully proficient at the heel and sit on the lead, then the heel-free exercise can be taught. Place the dog in the sit position, remove the lead, and as you step off, preferably with the left foot, give the command 'heel', encouraging the dog to follow by movements of the left hand as in the 'Heel' exercise on the lead. If he tries to move away from you, do not go after him or attempt any physical restraint – simply continue to attract his attention and call to him encouragingly.

If the dog has learned his heel-on-the-lead walk properly, there should be no difficulty, but even when he is working well when free, continue with occasional lead work and try to make the removal of the lead as matter-of-course and uneventful as possible so that the dog does not anticipate freedom and start to act boisterously. When working to heel off the lead, make frequent turns as before, encouraging the dog all the while and making it sit every time you come to a halt.

Eventually, on the command 'heel' the dog will walk freely at your side in the correct position, and without commands, signals or encouragement.

continued

section on the upper half of the rim. Modern pet-accessory suppliers often offer shapeless creations known as 'bean bags', made in various sizes and filled with polystyrene 'beans'; these can be comfortable beds for dogs of most breeds – as long as the beans cannot escape and the bags are large enough for the breed. For this former reason, and for cleanliness, it is useful to have a zip-cover made for the bean bag so that it can be regularly washed and brushed; also it will give added strength should the dog feel the need to drag the bag around the room. Other forms of bed are available from pet shops in a wide variety of shapes and sizes.

A dog's bed should be comfortable, of the right size to accommodate the dog when it is fully grown, contain bedding material which can be removed and washed or replaced periodically (and disinfected and allowed to dry in the sun if parasites are detected), be both warm and dry and positioned in a place free from draughts and constant noise but airy. Always have a change of clean bedding ready.

Quiet please

A good house dog is not one that starts barking at everyone and everything. If properly trained, he will be able to tell who should be around and who should not.

Encouraging your dog to keep quiet should form a part of his early training and if he also gets plenty of love and companion-ship he is unlikely to develop bad habits. Some breeds are, however, harder to quieten and you should bear this in mind when choosing a dog.

The 'Down' exercise – and looking happy about it

THE DOWN EXERCISE

The next stage is the down exercise. The dog must be sitting in the heel position on your left side and on the lead. Shorten the lead with your right hand, then place your left hand on his back just behind the shoulders. At the same time as you give the command 'down' – positively and with authority – pull the dog down with the lead and press him down with a backward movement of the left hand.

The word 'down' should be used alone – never say 'sit down' as the 'sit' and the 'down' are distinctly different movements. 'Lie down' is superfluous, 'down' being the operative command. It is always advisable especially in early training, to simplify commands as much as possible.

An alternative method of teaching the 'Down' exercise is to kneel in front of the dog and, holding the lead in the right hand close to the dog's neck, pull him into the down position while easing the forelegs forward with the left arm.

Spend sufficient time on the 'Down' exercise to ensure that the dog will respond instantly, but continue to practise the previous exercises also.

THE STAY EXERCISE

When a good level of proficiency in the previous basic exercises has been reached the foundation has been laid for teaching the pupil to remain in the 'Sit' or 'Down' position when the trainer walks away.

So far no hand signals have been used, but in this exercise, and in more advance work when the dog is at a distance from the trainer, signals are essential.

The 'Stay' exercise is commenced with the dog at heel in the 'Down' position and on the lead. Turn to face the dog, the lead in your left hand, and walk slowly backwards with the right arm in front of the body about chest height with the hand open and the palm towards the dog, at the same time giving the firm command 'stay'. If he remains in the down position without movement when the lead is fully extended, stand there for about a minute and then return to the dog, walking right round him, approaching his left side and again taking up the heel position on his right. Give praise, but be restrained as too much enthusiasm on your part at this stage may excite him to move or to get up. If, as you stand in front of him, he attempts to move or get up, pull him back into the 'Down' position with the lead accompanied by the command 'down' and followed by the appropriate signal and command for the 'stay'.

When there is a good response, the lead may be quietly placed on the ground in front of the dog and you can retreat a few yards further than before, remaining there a little longer. Then return to the dog after a few minutes if he has not moved, walk round him and again take up the 'Heel' position. Do not call the dog to you. Gradually increase the distance from the dog if good progress is being made, but do not go too far away nor remain away too long in the early stages. Eventually, the lead will be unnecessary, and instead of backing away while facing the dog, you will be able to place the dog in the 'down' position while at heel, give the command 'stay' and simply walk away. However, keep an eye on the dog to enable you to correct it instantly if it moves or attempts to get up.

This exercise can, of course, be extended to a stay in the 'Sit' position, teaching this on the lead initially, but as sitting is less comfortable than lying down it should not be held for long periods.

Try to vary the place in which you carry out the 'stay' exercise, otherwise the dog will associate it with a particular area and may not be as steady elsewhere. Later, distractions of people and animals walking nearby can be introduced, but always return to the dog. Recalling the dog from the 'stay' should not be practised until he is established in the exercise and totally reliable.

The 'Stay' exercise should be ended by your standing by your dog in the 'Heel' position, pausing a moment, then, taking a single step forward, bring the dog to the sitting-at-heel position with the command 'heel'. If well done you can now praise him lavishly, letting him see how pleased you are.

Do not neglect to continue with the previous exercises daily. Remember always to be patient, kind and firm; always be certain that the dog understands your commands and never administer reproof except for deliberate disobedience.

If the above principles are observed, you will soon be the owner of a well-behaved, alert, eager, obedient dog whose level of intelligence will have been improved by using his brain and who will always take pleasure in his work and be eager to please you.

The groundwork will now have been laid for more advanced training if you wish to proceed further, but in any case you will have transformed a young, untrained dog into a close companion and friend of whom you can feel justly proud.

If in any doubt regarding the health of your dog, if it seems at all 'off colour', or shows any sign of unusual behaviour, do not persist with training, but consult a veterinary surgeon without delay. If you are unable to afford private fees, go to your nearest PDSA animal treatment centre.

'Stay' – and the beginning of the hand signals used in advanced training

Lead pullers

Some dogs pull on their leads. This is usually from lack of training and is very difficult to correct. However, a wonderful invention is now available called a HALTI. It comes in several sizes, and acts rather like a halter. It is most effective, and much kinder than those chains which some people inflict on their dogs' necks.

Working Dogs

The first working dogs, as shown in prehistoric cave paintings, hunted alongside man for wild oxen, reindeer, stags and in northern areas seals and seabirds. Gradually, as the nomadic tribes settled down and began to rear stock and cultivate crops, dogs were employed to guard and herd the animals man had now domesticated. Hunting still continued, throughout the centuries, and hounds were still needed. Then, with the invention of firearms, gundogs were developed with different skills – to flush out the game and retrieve the kill, while (mostly in the British Isles) terriers were specially bred to deal with rats, foxes and other vermin.

DOGS OF WAR

The earliest British dogs seem to have been of one all-purpose shape and size, until the Celts arrived around 400BC. They were said to have been fond of dogs and skilled in breeding and training them. Dog lovers or not, the Celts did not hesitate to use their large fierce mastiffs as dogs of war, and the Gauls imported their dogs to use in the fight against Julius Caesar's invading armies.

Indeed, Caesar's reasons for invading Britain were quoted as, 'for gold, horses, hounds and skins'. Later Romans continued this tradition. The historian Pliny the Younger recorded the platoons of dogs which fought in the front of every battle; they were so brave that they never retreated unless ordered to do so. The Romans also used British dogs to guard their walls and fortifications and to carry messages. (They often forced the dog to swallow the message. On arriving safely at its destination, the dog was killed and cut open to retrieve the communication!) A popular saying in Rome was that the best thing about the British was their dogs. These were imported into Rome in large numbers to take part in the spectacles held in the arena of the Colosseum where they were set against wild animals, as well as men and women. Seven Scottish dogs who appeared in the games at the Circus Maximus were said to be of such ferocity that they could only be transported in cages like lions and tigers and the populace marvelled when they first set eyes on them.

Dogs continued to do war work well into this century, though in less violent ways. In the World War I they were trained to carry

---

Teddy and the train

In the country, of course, the working mongrel really does get the chance to prove his worth. Teddy Williams, an enchanting pre-war Rough Diamond, used to trot down to his master's chicken farm every day, climb the ladder to the nesting boxes, collect the eggs in a basket, and carry them a mile back to the house. He never broke one.

A train ran through his master's land, and the guard used to chuck the morning paper into the fields for Teddy to collect. Tragically, one day the guard forgot to throw it out. Perplexed, Teddy hared after the train, crossed in front of the train, losing a back leg and receiving a deep gash in the head. One of the local vets was called in to put him out of his misery, but when Teddy gazed up at him with pleading eyes, he said, 'I simply can't do it. The dog's in terrible pain, but he's begging me to save him.'

The vet was right. Teddy recovered with incredible speed, resumed his duties on three legs with as much gusto as ever and lived to be nineteen.

'Never too young to make friends'

messages in metal canisters attached to their collars. Dogs could negotiate shell craters and other obstacles faster and much more easily than soldiers, and being lower to the ground were less likely to be spotted by the enemy. Many were killed in the execution of their duties. Trained ambulance dogs saved many lives by seeking out wounded men often in the dead of night and in pitch darkness. Each dog carried on his back a small pack clearly marked with a Red Cross and containing a small bottle of brandy, bandages and other medicaments. If the wounded soldier was fit enough to move, the dog would guide him back to camp; if not the clever animal would go and bring help.

Opposite:
*Gundogs were developed to flush
out the game and retrieve the kill*

Dogs were also busy in World War II on active service and on the home front. There were the 'para dogs' dropped by parachute behind German or Italian lines, where they worked as patrol dogs for soldiers who had infiltrated enemy territory. Others crossed the Channel after D-Day to work as mine sniffers (a job dogs still do). Many of these brave dogs won the Dickin Medal 'For Gallantry' as did some of those who saved lives by finding people buried in bombed buildings.

The People's Dispensary for Sick Animals used to send their officers to look for pets injured or made homeless by the bombing, and one of them was always accompanied by his Wire Fox Terrier. One day the little bitch, Beauty, wandered off on her own and began digging in the rubble of a ruined building. Her owner soon became aware that she had discovered a cat buried alive under the debris. Realising that dogs could fulfil a vital function in saving human lives, the authorities set up a training unit and a skilled team was soon performing sterling work in the aftermath of the air raids. Two German Shepherds, from this team, Jet and Irma, marched proudly in the victory parade through the streets of London in 1946 and the immense cheer that greeted their appearance showed that the people had not forgotten their gallant efforts. Since then, dogs have been trained to search for earthquake and accident victims in all kinds of conditions.

MOUNTAIN RESCUE DOGS

For centuries, the St Bernard with a small keg of brandy round his neck has been the enduring and instantly recognisable symbol of a mountain rescue dog though, in fact, none of the dogs from the famous original St Bernard Hospice ever wore any keg containing any sort of spirits. So much for popular legend. Nowadays the breeds used for this work are more likely to be German Shepherds, Labradors or Border Collies. The Swiss Alpine Club began training these dogs in earnest just after World War II. Though the human eye could never see a skier or climber covered by drifting snow or trapped by an avalanche, a dog can soon find the missing person by scent. Being infinitely quicker and more accurate than any human, dogs save many man hours and it has been estimated that in winter conditions one dog is worth no less than twenty men.

In 1963, Hamish MacInnes, leader of the Glencoe Mountain Rescue Team, was invited by the Red Cross to watch a dog training session in Switzerland and he immediately realised that their work could be adapted to conditions in the hills of England, Scotland and Wales, at night and in poor visibility, as well as in snow. So SARDA (the Search and Rescue Dogs Association) was born, and divided into its three regional branches in 1971. Training is rigorous and only dogs with a good grounding in obedience can go on to specialised training. Their handlers must be qualified mountaineers. All this hard, dangerous, disciplined work is undertaken on a purely voluntary basis and most of the costs are borne by the handlers themselves. As they say, 'It is an unwritten law that every dog handler will answer a call for help at any time'.

ESKIMO DOGS

Since time immemorial, dogs have worked in the snow in the most hostile climates in the world. Eskimo dogs are capable of pulling sledges over enormous distances in temperatures well below zero and in winds of up to 100mph on a diet of dried meat and fish. Without them the Eskimo peoples could not have survived and Arctic and Antarctic expeditions would have been impossible. Malamutes (who hauled the heaviest freight), Eskimo Dogs and Siberian Huskies worked all over the vast frozen tundras of northern Asia, Canada, Greenland and Alaska when dogs were the only possible means of transportation.

Today, they are still highly prized for racing. In Alaska, dog-sled racing is the official state sport and the 1,000 mile Iditarod from Anchorage to Nome is known as 'The Last Great Race on Earth'. A similar event has recently been established in the Alps: the Alpirod covers 600 miles of mountain trails in Italy, France, Switzerland and West Germany. Our strict quarantine laws prevent British teams competing, but they have their own championships in Aviemore in Scotland.

DOGS IN HARNESS

Dogs have traditionally pulled carts in several northern European countries. Bernese Mountain Dogs hauled loads of dairy produce or baskets to market; similar dogs delivered milk in Belgium and flowers in Holland. Not in France, however, for the idea caused such outrage among the dog-loving French that it was forbidden by law by 1824.

As a nation of gourmets though, the French have always been happy to profit from the skills of the dogs who sniff for truffles, 'the diamonds of cooking'. Even Louis XV amused himself by searching for these delicacies with a team of specially trained dogs. Truffle dogs are still used, but other specialised working breeds became extinct when there was no longer any demand for their services, eg, medieval dogs who drew water from wells and turned spits for roasting meat. The work of the turnspit dog was hard and very hot; it took a long time for a large joint to cook so the bandy-legged little creatures had to run round their treadmill for many hours at a time. Most large houses or castles had two dogs working on alternate days. Each dog had his day (probably the origin of this famous old saying) and he always knew which it was. Slightly less arduous must have been the lot of the Tibetan breeds who were said to have turned prayer wheels in many monasteries in their native land.

PERFORMING DOGS

Most bands of strolling players had little dogs who walked on their hind legs, jumped through hoops, turned somersaults or pretended to be dead, as did most circuses until very recently. A troupe of poodles called 'The Ball of Little Dogs' delighted Queen Anne when they appeared before her in 1700.

One of the best music-hall dogs was 'Nino the Wonder Dog' who appeared in all the top theatres in support of great stars like Judy Garland. A black-and-white Fox Terrier type and a very skilled performer indeed, his special talent was to appear on stage by himself; no handler was ever seen. He loved his work and never missed a performance, to the great disappointment of his understudy, who was also his uncle.

Shakespeare wrote a part for a dog, Crab in *Two Gentlemen of Verona*. Others have achieved international stardom in films. A German Shepherd puppy was rescued from the World War I trenches by a US serviceman – and went on to become the legendary Rin-Tin-Tin, star of many silent films. Then there was Lassie (though there were many Lassies in every film, a different one for almost every scene.)

LAW AND ORDER

The intelligence, courage, toughness, tenacity, agility and obedience of the German Shepherd have made it the ideal police dog, though some forces have employed other breeds with success. Shepherds have been stabbed, shot, run over and sometimes killed in action; their record for devotion to duty is second to none. They are used wherever there are crowds to be controlled, football hooligans to be kept in order, criminals to be tracked down and arrested, frontiers to be patrolled or property and people to be guarded.

Around the world, armed forces rely heavily on dogs to guard installations, arms and munition depots, aircraft hangars and technical laboratories. Then there are the sniffer dogs who can find drugs and explosives, however cunningly they are concealed.

Car sickness

Most dogs travel well but some suffer from motion sickness. A dog should be familiarised with travel at an early age; if it appears to be getting distressed, or pants and salivates, stop to let it out of the car for a short time before continuing the journey. It also helps to have a passenger who will talk to the dog soothingly and gently calm it down. With these methods and a lessening of any fear the dog may have of the car, it usually grows out of the problem as it gets older.

In extreme cases, or those where the condition persists to the dog's frequent distress, consult a veterinarian who will probably prescribe tranquillisers to be taken before a journey.

Sniffers on parade

The ever vigilant Bill, a working Border Collie

DOGS AS SHEPHERDS

Nearly every country in Europe has developed its own pastoral breeds for guarding or driving the flocks and herds. Some have been adopted (and occasionally adapted) as show dogs and for obedience or agility competitions, but many are still rare even in their countries of origin and totally unknown outside of them.

Some of the larger breeds are undoubtedly descended from the Epirotic, Laconian and the Molossian dogs mentioned by Aristotle, later used by the Romans as war dogs. They in turn probably evolved from the great Mastiffs of Tibet – the Anatolian Sheepdog from Turkey is typical of these. The roll-call of working breeds is formidable. Egypt has the Armant; Israel the Canaan Dog; Russia four types of Owtcharki (called in Poland Owczarek), or Sheepdogs. Rumania and Yugoslavia each have their own sheepdog, plus the Croatian. Hungary has five distinct breeds; two of them the Komondor and the Puli (of the unique corded coat) are said to have been introduced by the Magyars when they emigrated from the steppes of Central Asia. From Italy comes the Bergamaschi Herder, the Maremma and the Italian Spitz. The German Shepherd dog (Alsatian) is the great all-purpose breed. France has four sheepdogs: the Beauceron, the Briard, the Picardy and the Pyrenean. Holland has two: the Dutch Sheepdog and the Schapendoes. Belguim has four: the Groenendael, the Lakenois, the Malinois and the Tervueren plus two Bouviers, de Flandres and des Ardennes. Switzerland is the home of four Sennenhunde or Mountain Dogs: the Appenzell, the Bernese, the Entlebuch and the Great Swiss. From Spain comes the popular Pyrenean Mountain Dog and the Catalonian Sheepdog; from Portugal, the Alentejo Herder, the Serra des Aires and the Castro Laboreiro sheepdogs, plus the Estrela Mountain Dog.

The Samoyed people living near the Arctic Circle developed the lovely breed which bears their name to tend their herds of reindeer. In Lapland, the Lapphund serves the same purpose. Norway has her Buhund, Sweden the Vastgotaspets or Vallhund and there is even an Icelandic Sheepdog. All five dogs belong to the Spitz group.

In Australia, where dogs were indispensible to work the huge flocks on vast ranges, over rough ground and often in extreme heat, breeds emerged that were as tough as the terrain, including the Kelpie to work with the sheep and the Australian Cattle Dog, a mixture of many breeds including the native wild dingo. The Australian Shepherd has nothing to do with the Antipodes but was bred in the USA from nearly all the old droving breeds. There are almost 50,000 hard at work in America though none of them are recognised by the AKC.

In Britain there is a long tradition of sheep and cattle dogs. The Bearded Collie's ancestor was the Polish Lowland Sheepdog or Owcarek Nizinny, much prized by Scottish farmers in the sixteenth century, but only recently reintroduced to Britain. The Old English Sheepdog is possibly also descended from Polish (or maybe Russian) sheepdogs, as are three Scottish breeds – the Rough and Smooth Collies and the smaller Sheepdog from the Shetland Isles.

Cattle were kept under control by the Welsh Cardigan and Pembroke Corgis (though the latter are now more at home in royal palaces), and by the Lancashire Heeler. These three breeds are obviously related to the Swedish Vallhund. Unequalled for working with sheep, the Border Collie is in a class of his own. Still universally used as a farm dog, since gaining Kennel Club recognition he is now popular for showing and obedience and work ability. Sheepdog Trials have become a popular sport as well as a way of life. The majority of guide dogs are Labradors or Labrador/Golden Retriever crosses.

The 'hearing ears' for the deaf scheme originated in the USA and came to Britain in 1982. These dogs can give to the profoundly deaf the same sort of independence that a Guide Dog gives to the blind. Dogs are trained to alert their deaf owners to any sound; a knock at the door, whistling kettle, alarm clock, fire alarm or crying baby.

Dogs are also being trained to help physically handicapped people by, for instance, switching lights on and off, bringing cordless telephones, opening and closing doors, picking things up from the floor and helping their owners to rise from chairs/wheelchairs or climb stairs.

Dew claw

The dog's fifth digit in rudimentary form; one appears on the inside of each leg. The origin of the name is obscure but it has been suggested that while all other claws touch the ground the dew claw merely brushes the dew from the grass. These claws, if left in place, tend to be a continual nuisance as they catch in undergrowth and in other objects when the dog is running or playing, causing painful tears in surrounding flesh. For this reason many veterinarians remove them shortly after birth, usually around the fourth day.

Dew claws that are left on and tear back should be gently bathed with a warm saline solution and bound to the leg until healed. If there is infection seek the advice of a veterinarian.

This cleverly trained spaniel tells his deaf owner that the kettle is boiling

PAT dogs bring delight to elderly patients

PAT DOGS

PAT (PRO-Dogs Active Therapy) Dogs make regular visits with their owners to old peoples' and childrens' homes, hospitals and hospices, giving pleasure to old, deprived, lonely or sick people of all ages. The scheme was the brain-child of the founder of the charity PRO-Dogs, Lesley Scott-Ordish, inspired, perhaps, by Psalm, a Longcoat Chihuahua who always accompanied his owner Nena Musker, when she gave classes in movement and community singing at several old people's homes in the London area. When the nursing staff saw how eagerly their residents looked forward to his visits; how they practically queued to pat and stroke him and give him little presents, they realised what a beneficial effect he was having. About the same time, there was news of the studies being carried out by Dr Aaron Kaatcher in the USA to prove that patting an animal has positive physical as well as psychological benefits.

The first PAT Dog, Sabre, a Rough Collie, was registered in 1983 and a pilot project got under way in Derbyshire. The scheme caught on at once, and now, in little more than half a decade there are at least as many PAT Dogs as Guide Dogs, if not more. These dogs really do enjoy their work, and their owners love to know that their dogs are appreciated and admired.

Many moving stories have emerged; the young man seriously disabled in a road accident who had no interest in living until a PAT dog appeared on the scene; the lonely old man who hadn't a single friend in the world until a particular dog began visiting; the physically handicapped young woman who would not attempt to move from her chair until she had a dog to take for a walk; and the very old lady whose last wish before her death was to see and stroke her beloved PAT dog just once more.

SAM THE POLICE DOG

One reason there are no mongrels in the police or the army is because they don't instantly symbolise authority. If you are about to start a riot or bash up an old lady, you're more likely to think again if an Alsatian or a Rottweiler comes pounding round the corner, rather than a lovable mongrel, however intelligent.

One senior policeman attached to the Hampshire force, however, did realise the full idiosyncratic potential of the mongrel, and decided to inject a note of comedy into the routine police dog displays. About six years ago he sent for PC Williams, one of his most experienced dog handlers, and told him to find a really scruffy but intelligent mongrel. Somewhat sceptically PC Williams set about this task and, having drawn a blank at all the local dog sanctuaries, took a train up to London to visit Battersea Dogs' Home.

'I sat down in this big compound,' said PC Williams, ' and lit my pipe, and had a good look at all the dogs that were milling around. Sam was the first one to come up and introduce himself. He was certainly one of the scruffiest, dirtiest animals I've ever seen, but he was also the most delightful, and although soon other dogs followed suit and came up and talked to me, I knew I couldn't go home without Sam.'

The only drawback was that once he got home, and was bathed and groomed at the police kennels, Sam turned into a very handsome dog, with merry amber eyes, a magnificent brown and white coat, and a plumed tail like an ostrich feather. Fortunately for his future he was as brainy as he was good-looking, and still retained his essential mongrel insouciance. He was also exceptionally quick to learn. He needed to be.

Less than seven weeks later, a large crowd including the Queen and the Duke of Edinburgh were gathered at Stratfield Saye, watching a group of police Alsatians giving an immaculate obedience display. Suddenly a disreputable-looking individual dressed in a dirty mac and a flat cap, with a jaunty brown and white mongrel on the end of a piece of string, dodged under the ropes, and had the impertinence to line up with the other dog handlers. A voice over the tannoy warned him to make himself scarce. Immediately an over-zealous security man in a 'hundred and fifty guinea check suit' charged up to the disreputable-looking individual and tried to frog-march him out of the ring.

'Beat it,' muttered PC Williams under his breath, 'Sam and I are part of the act.'

Next minute, to the ecstasy of the crowd, Sam was taking part in the display. Following PC Williams' orders, he did everything the other police dogs did, making up in exuberance anything he may have lacked in precision. Her Majesty and her husband were seen to be much amused.

So began Sam's remarkable career. Working alongside the police dogs, he took part in displays all over Hampshire, and stole the show wherever he went. When he did what he was told the crowd adored it, and if he occasionally slipped up, they enjoyed it even more. Alas, he was only allowed to delight his public for a year, at the end of which time, owing to the shortage of manpower, all police dog demonstrations were reluctantly discontinued. Poor Sam was forcibly retired and a shadow hung over his future. Luckily he had so endeared himself to PC Williams and his family by then that they adopted him as a family pet, and he is still keeping them amused by his antics.

Breeding

Opposite:
Kind, careful handling from an early age will ensure these two Cavalier pups a home for life

Below:
Mum – when we grow up, will we have beards like yours?

The decision to breed from your dog should not be taken lightly; certainly not until the following criteria have been met. The bitch must be healthy enough to run no risks during pregnancy. Your veterinarian should check her over before she is mated. There must be adequate space and facilities to keep the bitch and growing, agile, untrained puppies when the litter arrives and for at least two months afterwards. Every member of the litter must be assured of a good,

LOST PROPERTY . . . FOUND ON THE BARKING ROUTE

He started by taking a non-paying ride on a bus on the North Woolwich to Barking route. The conductor tried to put him off, but he just wouldn't budge and went onto Upton Park Garage. As he had no collar his next stop was the Lost Property Office, where he was given a label – DOG.

But you just can't stack away a dog like an umbrella, hat or briefcase so he ended up at Battersea, waiting for his owner to collect him. It didn't happen, but because he was healthy and fit he was soon found a new home.

Freddie Reed

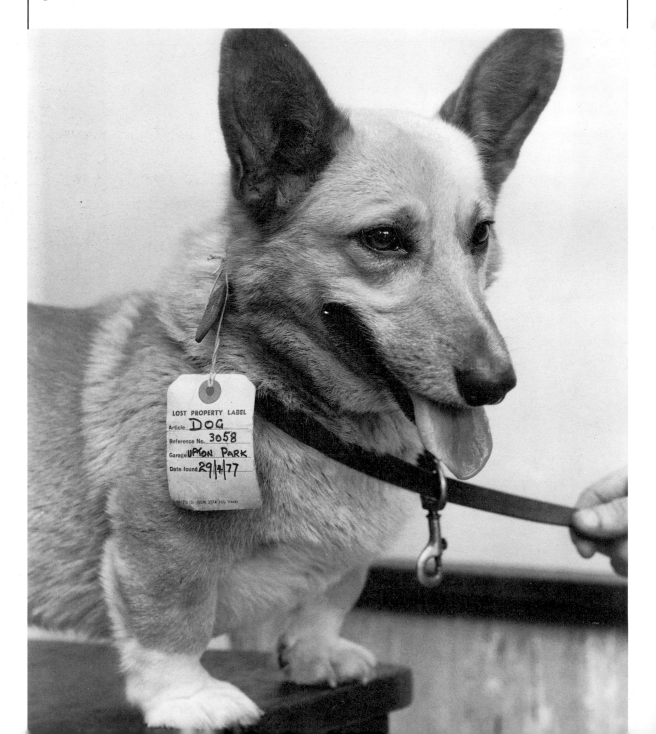

caring home for its full life. The dog chosen to sire the litter must not be related to the bitch, and neither bitch nor dog should be mentally or physically defective in any way.

Breeders of all kinds bear a heavy responsibility to ensure a safe, happy and healthy future for all puppies of a liaison. Only the healthiest and best points of the canine race should be bred on and the weakest points bred out. Weak, nervous, aggressive, unhealthy or otherwise defective dogs should not be mated, however attractive their appearance.

There are no fortunes to be made from breeding. Most reputable dog breeders are kindly people and kindness in their approach will preclude them from being wealthy as a result of breeding dogs! It is also worth reflecting on the vast number of unwanted and stray dogs awaiting a future in very many rescue homes such as Battersea throughout the country.

In theory, a bitch can be mated following her first season, but it is best left until she is at least fifteen months old, or after her third season. A bitch over six years of age should generally be considered too old for her first litter. If your bitch has a fine pedigree you will probably have no difficulty in finding a suitable dog. The breeder of your own bitch, or the Kennel Club can help to find a suitable male.

A fine litter of pups enjoy a game in their own special corner

Collecting a new puppy

If you are making a longish journey to collect your puppy, try to collect it early in the day so that you reach home before dark. Strange shadows can startle a small puppy. Fear is to be avoided at all costs at this early stage. Leaving dam and siblings is stressful enough, so please be gentle, quiet and soothing.

A bitch is most likely to accept a dog for mating in the second stage of her season, at some time between the tenth and fifteenth day. The exact time varies between individuals and needs close observation to note a sideways movement of the tail when she is approached by the male dog or stroked gently down her loin. Mating requires supervision, especially with inexperienced animals, and space in which to move around. Dog and bitch should be introduced on leads until they become used to each other. After entering into the mating 'tie', the pair may turn back-to-back and hold this position for twenty minutes or more before muscular relaxation allows a gently parting. Any attempt to part them forcibly is very dangerous. Confirmation of the pregnancy cannot be made until about the fortieth day after mating (by a veterinarian). Make sure the bitch is checked over again as her pregnancy progresses.

False pregnancies sometimes occur, whether or not the bitch has been mated. Symptoms are 'nest-building', an enlarged abdomen and even a slight secretion of milk. A veterinarian should be consulted in such situations, as there may be unhealthy after-effects.

The gestation period is usually sixty-three days though this may vary by a day or so. Preparations should be made for the arrival of the puppies well in advance. You will need to consider who is to supervise whelping and be responsible for aftercare; then there is special accommodation, feeding and veterinary attendance. The bitch will also need more attention during these days of waiting: while the quantity of her food should not be increased, the quality is

YOUR DOG'S FAMILY TREE

One of the fascinating things about owning a pure-bred dog is its pedigree. Your dog's pedigree may only show 3, 4 of 5 generations, depending on the energy and enthusiasm of the breeder when he or she wrote it out, but it should be possible to trace it back very much further.

Your pedigree dog should be registered with the Kennel Club, in which case it has a KC number, and for a small fee the KC will issue a 3 generation pedigree. This, we hope, merely confirms the hand-written pedigree which came with your dog. Over the years, of course, names can be mis-spelt, mis-read and misplaced but it is sensible to start off with an accurate pedigree. Unless you have an obscure imported breed, in which case the pedigree names are often quite unpronounceable, the next thing to do is borrow or otherwise acquire as many books on your breed as possible. This way you will be able to read about the dogs behind yours, and possibly see photographs of them. If you become a member of the breed society, you will be able to discover the addresses of various breeders to whom you could write (not forgetting to enclose a stamped addressed envelope) asking for details and pedigrees of dogs that interest you. If you don't know who is the secretary of your breed society, ask the breeder who sold you your dog or, failing that, ask the KC. Breeders usually register their puppies under their own affix, so it is possible to discover who bred a certain dog by the way it is named. This is not infallible, however. If you become a member of your breed society you may be able to acquire old Year Books, which are extremely interesting. Kennel Club Stud Books are also full of information for pedigree researchers, as are the old Kennel Club Gazette Breed Records Supplements.

When some of the long established breeders reply to your letters, you often learn all sorts of interesting things about individual dogs, and you realise how much of a personality was a particular dog. You can become really 'hooked' on this pedigree research business. Apart from the fact that you are learning more about your breed, you are making contact with knowledgeable people, and you may be making some good friends.

important. Milk will be especially beneficial and there may be a need to add vitamins to her diet, particularly vitamins A and D. Exercise should not be curtailed but neither should it be strenuous.

When whelping time arrives, the mother-to-be needs a ready-prepared, familiar place which is quiet, draught-free and comfortable where she can deliver her puppies without disturbance. The ideal temperature is 24-30°C (70-75°F) when the pups are about six days old.

As the bitch nears delivery time, labour pains begin with slight straining, increasing to three or four contractions every three minutes or so. The water bag appears and breaks, then the first puppy's head soon makes an appearance. If no puppy has appeared after about an hour there may be complications which will require the presence of a veterinarian. Puppies usually appear at about fifteen or twenty minute intervals, though there are individual variations.

Above all, the mother (and her litter when they arrive) will need peace and quiet. Puppies are born blind with the umbilical cord still attached. This will be bitten through by the mother, or dam, as she is now called. One placenta follows each puppy. Note each one carefully to make sure that none are retained. If any are retained, call the veterinarian as an injection will be required to prevent infection. If the dam wishes to eat the placenta she should not be discouraged from doing so as the hormones contained in the placenta can help to clear the uterus of harmful debris.

After whelping the dam should be encouraged to drink a little milk mixed with a teaspoonful of honey or medicinal glucose. She should

We can't go another step . . .

Pencils

Puppies find pencils and crayons irresistible to chew. Many contain aniline dyes, however, (as does shoe polish) which destroys the haemoglobin of the blood. Symptoms of poisoning include vomiting, apathy and sometimes convulsions. A dog which has ingested aniline in this way may need its stomach washed out by a veterinarian, and oxygen and/or a blood transfusion may be necessary, together with drugs.

Chewed pencils can also be a potential hazard as foreign bodies. Pieces can become lodged in the throat, oesophagus or intestine causing damage and obstruction.

then be left with her new family to rest. This is not the time for a procession of friends and neighbours to see the new arrivals. No strangers should be allowed near them for at least two days and, if the dam resents intrusion then, her peace should be permitted to continue. She will also need building up with a specially nutritious diet to recover from the substantial shock to her system. For at least twenty-four hours after whelping she will need a liquid diet including, for example, beef broth, or a mixture of milk, water and honey or glucose. Feed about five times in this period.

Unless her temperature is abnormal or there are other complications about which your veterinarian will advise, the liquid diet may be alternated on the second day with light foods such as scrambled egg

Choking

This is an extremely dangerous condition which often proves fatal. Choking is frequently caused by a foreign body being partially swallowed and becoming lodged in the entrance to the trachea, thus blocking the supply of air to the lungs.

Prevention lies in not feeding the dog unsuitable bones and ensuring that all potentially hazardous small objects are kept out of its (and especially a puppy's) reach. Cure, if it is possible, must be the very speedy removal of the obstruction to allow the dog to breathe again. This is done by grasping the dog's tongue and pulling it forward and then attempting to pull out the foreign body with fingers, forceps or tweezers. The dog will be extremely distressed as it fights for breath and the fingers may be bitten. However, drastic measures are necessary to give the dog any chance of recovery.

'Choking' is also used as a term to describe an obstruction of the oesophagus, producing symptoms which include vomiting, refusal of food and dejection. Here there will be time to call for the advice of a veterinarian.

and brown bread, boiled bone-free fish or lightly cooked beef mince. As she recovers, build up her strength and health with good-quality beef (raw or almost raw but chopped), supplemented with raw or scrambled eggs. This, with regular drinks of cold water, will provide strength and build the milk supply. After the pups are weaned, fluid in meals can be reduced and her diet reinforced regularly with fresh meat, eggs, a good-quality biscuit meal, brown bread etc. Weaning can begin at about three or four weeks. Offer the puppies soft, wet foods which they will gradually learn to lap from shallow dishes (after a messy start). They will continue to suckle while being weaned until they are around five or six weeks of age, when more solid food can be introduced in four meals a day.

Eyes down for a full tummy . . .

Rescue

In Britain today there are literally hundreds of rescue organisations; The Dogs Home Battersea, The National Canine Defence League, with its kennels all over the country, Wood Green Animal Shelters in Hertfordshire and Cambridge, The Blue Cross, and many more. They vary from people who care and rehome from their own premises to the vast kennels housing hundreds of dogs and cats. At this moment there are thousands of dogs behind bars through no fault of their own, waiting for someone to offer them love and security. For every scrap of affection offered, they will repay a thousand times over. Walk down the rows of cages, and there is more love in the wistful, trusting, often merry, eyes, than we should find in many human beings.

Those of us who have spent a lifetime with pedigree dogs have sometimes been heard to remark that certain dogs are 'only mongrels', but this is so often unfair. Take Scruffy, for instance.

It would be a total impossibility to assess Scruffy's antecedents.

She is 'sort-of' pepper-and-salt, with a 'sort-of' longish coat. Her eyebrows stand out with the questioning look of a Schnauzer, or maybe an Airedale. One ear belongs to her, and the other to someone entirely different. Her tail comes from an indeterminate forebear and just doesn't fit. Neither do her feet, which were made for a much larger creature, with much heftier legs than her long spindles. She has a bit of so many breeds in her that she must be the world's foremost outcross, and at a year old she had already had numerous homes when she arrived at the local dog sanctuary via the police.

Above and opposite:
Restored to health by The National Canine Defence League

135

DOGS IN ANCIENT CIVILISATIONS

The first pictorial representations of the man/dog partnership showed the two combining as a hunting team. Rock paintings from the Bronze Age show men armed with bows and arrows, and spears made from antlers, and a pack of a dozen or so hunting dogs. France, Sweden and Spain all have evidence that Neolithic man and the dog hunted wild boar and deer. In Africa one of the finest series of rock paintings yet discovered shows vivid scenes of hunting wild oxen and ostriches in what was the then fertile region of the Sahara.

In Ancient Egypt the dog played an important part in the religious life of the community and was therefore shown in murals, tomb paintings and sculpture. The Egyptians were skilled hunters, animal breeders and agriculturists. The god Anubis symbolised both the dog and the jackal; bronze statues of Anubis show the lean head and large upright ears of one of the Mediterranean greyhounds. By 5000BC several varieties of dog were being painted with some accuracy. Most of these were of course hunting dogs, but Egyptian art also shows very tiny dogs whose only function could only have been as amusing playthings. The greyhound, the fastest of dogs bred by man, was developed in Ancient Egypt and murals of hunting scenes show both the drop-eared type like the modern Saluki and the upright-eared ones resembling the Pharaoh hound. Later bas reliefs and painted caskets show mastiffs but these were almost certainly brought to Egypt by invading armies. The dog is shown throughout Ancient Egyptian art as a hunter, a dog of war and a companion animal, but never as a herding animal or a guard for the flocks.

The impressive Assyrian mastiffs from the walls of the palace of Assurbanipol at Nineveh (Courtesy of the British Museum)

Some of the most artistically satisfying portrayals of dogs from the pre-Christian era are found in the bas reliefs decorating the palace of Assurbanipol at Nineveh. These show the Assyrian mastiffs which became famous throughout the Mediterranean region for their size, strength and courage. King Assurbanipol is shown going hunting after lion, wild horses and smaller game which required the nets carried by his servants. His dogs are led from the palace on rope slip leads or wearing coiled copper collars. They are majestic in size, superbly muscled and fit, and with the broad powerful muzzle characteristic of the mastiff group. Later scenes show them pulling down horses and attacking lions. There is no doubt they were also used in war to pull down the enemy troops. From such animals are descended some of today's giant breeds.

Homer's *Odyssey* relates one of the most famous of dog stories, that of the faithful Argus, a favourite hound of Odysseus. Old, neglected, lying on the dunghill at the gate, Argus was the only one to recognise Odysseus on his return home after a nineteen year absence, and the joy of recognition killed him.

We know from the pictures of ancient Greek hounds that the quarry included boar, stags and hares. There was a profound difference between these hound breeds developed in the lands north of the Mediterranean and those hunting dogs used by the peoples of Egypt and North Africa. The Greek hounds were expected to be fast but they were also valued for their ability to follow a scent. The Egyptian dogs were faster still but hunted mainly by sight, a disadvantage in wooded and moist areas. Poems and epitaphs show that the Greeks valued dogs for their companionship and as pets. Toy dogs had already made their appearance to delight and amuse. In the legends that have come down to us some themes recur. One is of the hunter being devoured by his own pack of hounds, sometimes as a punishment for having offended the gods: Actaeon was torn to pieces by his own hounds for having surprised the goddess Diana bathing.

Though the Romans valued hunting hounds, their statuary, pottery and mosaics also showed watchdogs, sheep and herding dogs and dogs of war. They admired dogs of courage and valour prepared to defend their master's property to the death. Pliny quotes various anecdotes showing the dog's fidelity and devotion to duty. He also tells us that the Romans ate dogs, whose flesh was considered to have medicinal qualities, and sacrificed them to their gods at various religious festivals. The Romans described, for the first time, the dogs of Europe. The wolfhounds of Gaul and the mastiffs of Britain were recorded with admiration and brought back to Italy as part of the conquering armies' plunder.

Young as she was, Scruffy had had more than a lifetime's share of cruelty. Yet from all of her indeterminate, ill-fitting features her lovely eyes shone out with incredible beauty. Dogs cannot speak with their voices, but dogs like Scruffy do not need to. Their eyes tell the whole story.

A young family took over the village Post Office, and were told they ought to have a 'guard dog'. Neither partner had ever lived with a dog, nor did they have any idea about feeding or training. It did seem sensible, however, to get a 'good guard', and the most likely place was the local dogs home. Off they went with the two children down the rows of pens with their eager occupants. In spite of a few pedigrees and those with recognisable guarding antecedents, the children fell for Scruffy. No other dog would do. Sad and frightened, she did not look much like a guard dog, but she was the choice. Needless to say, there were some teething problems (as is generally the case with rehomings, particularly with a family which has never owned a dog), but Scruffy trained herself and her people, and nobody could have a more clever, obedient, alert guard.

Scruffy, of the ill-assorted personal attributes and beautiful eyes, found happiness and security. Fortunately her story is typical of many, and this makes it possible for the rescuees to go on facing all the sadness and neglect. The lovely people offering lovely homes cheer the hearts and strengthen the will of everyone involved in this sad work.

Above:
'I may not be pedigree but I'm full of beans'

Left:
These two healthy mongrels were rescued after being abandoned on the motorway

Unwanted gifts

Never buy a dog as a present for someone else unless that someone knows all about it and definitely wants it. Also, never buy a dog at Christmas, when parties abound, strangers visit and there is so much excitement in the air. A dog or puppy coming into a new home needs a stable environment and time to settle in before celebrations disturb the peace.

Help is at hand – The People's Dispensary for Sick Animals comes to the rescue

Opposite:
Rescued dogs often make superb pets, repaying every scrap of affection many times over

By far the highest proportion of dogs coming into sanctuary are mongrels or crossbreeds. There are, however, increasing numbers of pedigree dogs. One reason for this is the existence of 'puppy farms', where numerous bitches are kept and bred from every season, often in unsuitable conditions, the offspring being sold through petshops and dealers. Another reason for too many pedigree dogs coming onto the market is the great popularity of the show ring. Every enthusiastic exhibitor wants to continue showing, but the showing life of a dog is very short. It is necessary therefore to have a new puppy to bring out, regularly, and, for every puppy kept for the ring, there are five, six, seven, ten to put onto the market. All these excess puppies add to the numbers jostling for the good homes available on the market – the homes where a dog will be loved and cherished FOR LIFE.

Also, more people are opting for the big, guarding breeds which need space, exercise and special training. Unfortunately, the people who buy them often do not have the lifestyle to suit them, and many become unmanageable through no fault of their own. As a result, some are thrown out on the motorway, on commonland, jettisoned in the park, or maybe just cast out on the streets.

Unsuitable people, unsuitable life-style, unsuitable dogs – a picture repeated thousands of times over, the length and breadth of Britain.

The rescue or rehoming of pedigree dogs used to be handled easily by caring owners and the breed clubs, but to handle the increased need breed rescue organisations have been set up. In some cases, where the need is small, they are run by individuals. Other breeds have well organised groups, often registered charities with representatives throughout the whole of Britain; often working full stretch to take in and rehome the unwanteds. Such people do it all voluntarily and the work often costs them dear. Seeing so much sadness, it is rare for people involved in breed rescue to continue breeding dogs!

Another needy dog receives care and attention at The National Canine Defence League, Petersfield

138

The Dog
and the Law

Since this book is for people who love dogs it is clearly unnecessary to draw their attention in detail to those legal provisions which deal with ill-treatment or cruelty to their pets. On the other hand, a general statement might help them to recognise occasions when the law ought to be invoked against others.

Apart from that aspect of the law it is important to realise that dog ownership, or merely guardianship if one is looking after a friend's pet, carries with it certain clearly defined legal obligations. Those obligations are to society in general, other members of the public and, when one is in the country, to the farming community in particular.

ACQUIRING A DOG

When you buy a dog, the position in law is just the same as when buying any other chattel or piece of merchandise; the seller is deemed to have the right to sell. If he does not have the right to sell he is liable to an action for breach of contract. There is no sort of warranty implied that the dog is fit for any particular purpose, though this might arise if the buyer made known the purpose at the time of buying and was assured on the point.

When dealing with breed dogs, the authenticity of any pedigree referred to becomes a part of the contract. If a buyer is the victim of a deliberate fraud by the seller, he may return the animal and sue for his money, or he may keep it and claim damages.

If you are given a dog, clearly, no such questions arise. If you are looking after a dog for its owner then, in his absence, you have all the rights and obligations of ownership, subject of course to any specific instructions from the owner and to returning the animal when demanded.

If you find a dog which appears to be a stray with no means of identification, you must take it to the nearest police station. Failure to do so is an offence. You will be permitted to keep it (if you wish), unless it is claimed by the owner within seven days. If you do opt to keep it, you must do so for at least a month. The law relating to stray dogs is to be found in the Dogs Act 1906 and the Dogs (Amendment) Act 1928.

So you have acquired your dog by one means or another; what

other formalities are now obligatory?

From every point of view, and not merely to comply with the law, the absolute priority at the moment of acquisition is a collar with your name and address on it (or on a badge or plate attached to it). Everybody knows the problem of stray dogs with no form of identification. These largely belong to owners who do not care sufficiently to try to trace them or who have deliberately abandoned them. But even owners who do care enough to search for their lost dogs go through a harrowing experience – to say nothing of the dog's experience. Then there are those strays which cannot be claimed because they are killed in traffic accidents or kept by a finder. So, never let your dog run collarless if there is the remotest chance that it could escape. It is an offence so to do. The exceptions to this law are: packs of hounds, sporting dogs while so acting, sheep dogs and dogs used to destroy vermin, while so doing.

Experiments are currently being undertaken on a permanent and ineradicable form of identification for dogs; a minute painless injection, giving the animal its own 'readable' code signal which can be recorded on a central computer. Much remains to be resolved administratively, but the potential benefits are obvious.

What about a licence? At the time of writing, this is no longer required. After many years during which the revenue raised from the

The absolute priority is a collar with your name and address attached

141

annual dog licence requirement fell far short of the cost of recovering it, the government gave up the struggle (due no doubt partly to disinclination to lose votes by raising the fee to a realistic level). Such a rise would now result in an annual fee of perhaps £20. It should be noted, however, that the power to re-introduce a licence has been retained. If you are in the guard dog business you do require a licence from the local authority – not for your dogs but for your kennels. The same is true for running a pet show or boarding kennels.

Every dog owner should also be aware of the law to protect against rabies: dogs imported into the UK must be held in quarantine for a specified period.

YOUR DOG'S BEHAVIOUR

You are responsible for your dog's behaviour. This covers a very wide spectrum perhaps the most obvious aspect being any behaviour affecting one's neighbours.

The keeping of animals so as to cause material discomfort or annoyance to anyone is a nuisance. If the matters complained of are sufficient to affect the health, comfort or convenience of the public in general then it amounts to a public nuisance, which is often covered by statute and punishable by a magistrates' court. If not so covered then the public's interests are looked after by the Attorney General, who may take the offending owner to court.

Normally the nuisance will not be so extensive and will be confined to immediate neighbours, in which case a civil action may result with an injunction ordering its cessation coupled perhaps with damages. The court will attempt to consider what is 'reasonable' concerning the rights of the owner and the complainant, and will take into account the kind of district involved. The obvious answer for the owner of boisterous dogs is to exercise them outside adequately, not to leave them alone too long and if possible choose a dog lover as neighbour. In any event, avoid litigation; it is an expensive luxury.

Another aspect of controlling your dog's behaviour may well concern its temperament. Under the Dogs Act 1871, a court may hear complaints against dogs accused of being 'dangerous' and not kept under proper control. If a court considers this proven it may order the dog to be kept under proper control or destroyed. The court may order destruction without giving the owner the option of exercising proper control, but there is a right of appeal to the Crown Court. The court cannot order the dog's immediate destruction if the dog has genuinely acquired a new owner since the events complained of.

'Dangerous' does not mean dangerous to mankind only. Where a dog is proved to have chased or injured cattle or poultry it can be treated as a dangerous dog. Whether or not a dog is under proper control is a question of fact. There is no offence in merely keeping a dangerous dog – there must also be a failure of proper control. A dog may be classed as dangerous and not under control on the owner's own property to which other persons on lawful business have access. This does not exclude using one's dog to chase off intruders or trespassers, but bears particular reference to such as the unfortunate

---

The dog in fiction

At the end of the nineteenth century a number of highly successful fictional biographies of dogs began to appear. One was *Owd Bob* by Arthur Ollivant, published in 1898, which ran into many editions. Equally popular was Jack London's *Call of the Wild* followed by Sir Percy Fitzpatrick's *Jock of the Bushveld*. The logical successor to these three tales must be Eric Knight's *Lassie Come Home*, published in 1940 and progenitor of the classic film and innumerable television series.

In the picture

George Stubbs, one of Britain's foremost animal painters, was most famous for his eighteenth-century paintings of racehorses and foxhounds, but his pictures also show a whole catalogue of different dog breeds and throw interesting light on the kind of dogs kept by the landed gentry. Greyhounds, poodles, water spaniels, setters, pointers, various spitz and all types of land spaniel are shown against the rural landscapes of pre-industrial England.

Like father like son . . . Schnauzer and pup

postman or milkman.

There are also offences involving the bad behaviour of your dog in a street or public place in an urban district 'to the obstruction, annoyance or danger' of the residents or passers-by. These are: permitting to be at large 'any unmuzzled ferocious dog'; setting on or urging any dog to attack, worry or put in fear any person or animal, and offences connected with rabies.

One of the most unattractive and serious forms of bad canine behaviour for which the owner is legally liable is the worrying of livestock on agricultural land. The owner of the livestock can recover damages for his loss, and the dog's owner may be convicted and fined under the Dogs (Protection of Livestock) Act 1953. In this case, livestock includes cattle, sheep, goats, swine, horses and poultry. 'Agricultural land' includes market gardens, allotments, nursery grounds and orchards. 'Worrying' means attacking or chasing so that injury, suffering, abortion in females, or loss or diminution in produce might reasonably be expected to result. It is a defence if the livestock are trespassing and the dog is owned by or in charge of the owner of the land trespassed upon, provided he does not cause the dog to attack.

Moreover, the owner of livestock is entitled to shoot a dog when necessary to protect his own animals (but not game). For such shooting to be justified, the dog must be attacking the livestock or likely to renew the attack if left at large. It is not legal to lay down poison or a spring gun or set any baited trap to attract a dog.

It is interesting to note how far the law has developed over the centuries in respect of trespassing animals – including dogs. In Saxon times there was the attitude that the dog rather than the owner had to

DOGS IN THE COUNTRYSIDE

The behaviour of dogs in the countryside is probably the one single area where a dog owner is most likely to run into conflict with other people. Farmers, rightfully, can become very annoyed if dogs worry livestock, especially during the lambing or calving season. However, the possible dangers are no reason to avoid the pleasures of country walks as it is normally possible to control your dog in the open provided that it has been properly trained.

Safety first – keep him on the lead
Whenever you are walking in the country and you think that you may come across livestock, it is best to keep your dog on a lead. You may not be able to see any but your dog will be able to smell them and he can almost certainly run further and faster than you. You are quite entitled to let your dog off the lead in open countryside and natural parkland or anywhere else where you are sure there are neither livestock nor gamebirds.

Keeping your dog occupied
If you habitually follow the same route on your country walk, this can be boring for your dog and he may wander off in search of an interesting diversion. If possible, you should vary your route and also take a ball with you for your dog to play with.

Big dogs run further
If you have a long-legged dog which needs a good long run to let off steam, it is important to select your exercise areas with care. Try to find an area where there is absolutely no livestock, unfenced moorland for example, or ask a local farmer where a safe area might be.

If you usually exercise your dog in town, you will appreciate the need for using a lead. This discipline is just as necessary in the country but in order to allow your dog a little more freedom, it is as well to take a second and longer, country lead

Dogs, gamebirds and deer
It is just as important to keep dogs under control where game or other livestock is at large as it is to guard against injury to sheep and cows.

Pheasants are expensive to rear and the consequences of an attack by a dog can be just as serious as an attack on farm animals. Pheasants are by nature great wanderers and one of the most difficult tasks for the gamekeeper is to keep the birds in coverts (special hides for gamebirds). A dog chasing these birds may not kill or injure any of them but frightened birds will probably flee their coverts and not return. Gamebirds normally belong to someone who rears them professionally and who is entitled to be just as annoyed as a farmer if his investment is destroyed by a rampaging dog. And he may well have an action at law against the owner of the dog.

The consequences of a dog frightening large animals such as deer can be considerably worse. Startled deer may dash across public roads and become a menace to other walkers or to traffic.

As well as the dangers to livestock, dogs can make themselves unpopular with farmers by running through standing crops and by digging holes. Neither of these activities will endear your dog to the farmer, so it is up to you to curb any inappropriate tendencies that your dog may display.

The Golden Rule is that you will be able to prevent a well trained dog from annoying animals in the countryside if he or she comes to heel when you give the command.

THE COUNTRY CODE FOR DOGS

Prepared in consultation with the National Farmers' Union and the Countryside Commission

- Take your dog to training classes to learn elementary obedience.

- Keep your dog on a lead until you are confident that he is under control and keep the lead on at all times where there are farm animals.

- Never allow your dog to chase anything – it is a habit which is hard to break.

- Never allow your dog out on his/her own – and make sure you know where he/she is at all times.

- Keep your dog off cultivated fields.

- Know what to do in the case of an accident happening to your dog in a place where veterinary attention is not immediately available.

- Study the Country Code for yourself, and train your dog in country awareness.

be punished, although the 'punishment' of killing the dog inevitably affected the owner too. Thus the law of King Ine (688-695) provided: 'If any beast breaks hedges and wanders at large within, since its owner will not keep it under control, he who finds it on his cowland shall take it and kill it'. . .

This was known from ancient times as the 'lex talionis' or the law of vengeance, but over the centuries there arose the more humane idea of seizing the trespassing animal and 'impounding' it as security for any damage it had caused. In theory this remedy, known as 'distress damage feasant' still exists, but it is of more application when cattle or other livestock trespass and cause damage.

The lesson for dog owners is clear, whatever historical legal remedies survive. Always control your dog in the country and remember the farmer's right to shoot a dog attacking his livestock. It will be small comfort if a court decides later that the farmer was not justified.

Lastly under this heading one should mention the dog's behaviour in the street and other public places such as parks. Many local authorities now have bye-laws which seek to control the defecations of dogs, placing responsibility firmly on their owners – precisely where it should be. Such bye-laws often include a provision that in certain areas dogs shall at all times be kept on a lead. Apart from the penalties involved if a dog owner is caught breaching these laws, he/she may be liable if an unleashed dog were to run into the road and cause an accident. If the dog has gone out from home on its own the legal position may be different.

Dutch interiors

Dutch portrait painters frequently included dogs in their loving recreation of the interiors of their patron's houses. In the works of such painters as Frans Hals, Jan Steen and Pieter de Hoogh, we see dogs in a hundred natural poses; asleep, being fondled by their owners, stealing the cat's dinner, hunting for fleas, and joining, rather inappropriately, in a musical evening. Amongst the recognisable breeds in these seventeenth-century Dutch paintings are greyhounds, poodles and spaniels.

RIGHTS OF OWNERSHIP

If his dog is harmed in any way an owner can bring an action for damages in respect of the injury in the same way as he can for himself, his car or any other property. He may sue for its recovery against anyone in wrongful possession of it and it will remain his property even when lost or straying.

As has already been pointed out, however, once a dog is picked up as a stray and reaches a police station, the owner has the very limited time of seven days to claim it before it may be sold or destroyed.

CRUELTY

The general provisions of the Protection of Animals Act 1911, with its later amending Acts, applies to dogs as well as to other animals. These make it an offence for anyone to perpetrate or (in the case of the owner) allow someone also to perpetrate any of the following acts:

a) cruelly to beat, kick, ill-treat, torture, infuriate or terrify;
b) causing unnecessary suffering by doing or omitting to do any act;
c) conveying or carrying in such a manner as to cause unnecessary suffering;
d) performing any operation without due care and humanity;
e) fighting or baiting of dogs or the use of any premises for the purpose;
f) administering of any poisonous or injurious drug or substance.

By the Abandonment of Animals Act 1960, it is an offence for an owner or anyone in charge of or having control of an animal to abandon it without reasonable cause or excuse (one wonders what

About beds

Your puppy's first bed will probably be a cardboard box. Having been used to the other puppies snuggling up to one another, it would feel cold and frightened in a big dog bed. Don't give a bean bag to a puppy – it will only want to investigate it more closely, and you don't want it to eat the polystyrene beads! Do keep the bedding clean. Vetbed is the best, though it takes days to dry. Blankets tend to get chewed.

Three characterful German Shepherd pups with a future as crime busters

possible excuse there could be!) in circumstances likely to cause it unnecessary suffering, or to permit it (if the owner) to be so abandoned.

Any punishment for these offences can also involve an order disqualifying the person concerned from having custody of any animal or any of a specified kind.

The above are but the primary legal provisions in merest outline so far as they might affect the average dog owner. There are many other pieces of legislation affecting dogs of specialised kinds, eg, provisions for licensing pet shops and boarding establishments, provisions relating to performing animals and the exhibition of film scenes involving suffering, and provisions relating to animal experimentation. But with such matters the happy and caring dog owner has no direct concern.

Tales of Courage

MONGRELS AT WAR

Nowhere do mongrels show up to greater advantage than in war. One thinks not only of the valour which enabled them to bag six out of the sixteen dog VCs issued in the Second World War, but also of the way they remain cheerful under the most horrific circumstances.

To examine their valour first, we must start at the beginning of the Second World War when the public were invited to lend their dogs for the war effort. Well aware how devoted the British are to their animals, the War Office was pessimistic about the response and laid on a skeleton staff. Within a few days this staff was buckling under offers from more than 7,000 owners, asking only that their beloved animal should be given the chance to prove its worth.

Among many heartbreaking letters was one which said, 'My husband has gone, my son has gone, please take my dog to bring this cruel war to an end.'

Not many of the dogs submitted were suitable. They needed a sanguine temperament and a keen sense of smell. Mongrels were avoided on the whole because of the usual argument that they were unpredictable. The ones that did get through all looked vaguely like breed dogs. A good example was a Family Circler of exceptional courage called Bob. After his training, he was attached to 'C' Company of the 6th Royal West Kents and went with the regiment to North Africa where he excelled at carrying messages, guarding stores, and accompanying recce patrols. Bob won his Dickin Medal (the Dogs' Victoria Cross) at Green Hill, when with his white patches camouflaged with dark paint he led a night patrol into enemy lines. Suddenly he froze in his tracks. The patrol waited, and then, seeing nothing ahead, ignored the dog's warning and decided to push on. Bob refused to budge. Next second movement was discerned in the faint light 200 yards ahead. Bob had saved the patrol from almost certain capture or death.

This gallant mongrel went right through the Sicilian and Italian campaigns, and in cold weather wore a warm coat embroidered with the regimental crest. Tragically, while being retired to England to be re-united with his demobbed master, Bob slipped his collar in Milan and was never seen again.

Opposite:

Rare lad, is Cassidy

When this lovable rascal arrived at Battersea the kennel hands could hardly believe their eyes: he had only three legs. Promptly dubbed Cassidy, he was given all the care and attention he needed, and was put up for sale when he had not been claimed. Obviously his previous owner had lavished proper veterinary attention on him, as he had undergone a very expensive amputation operation which had helped him overcome his disability well. Cassidy was quickly found a new home and is now enjoying life to the full . . . even with three legs.

Freddie Reed

Royal duties

Back in the twenties, another
little mongrel called Monty Trott
ambitiously established himself
as resident guard dog at the
Tower of London. Given as a
puppy to the newly appointed
curator of the crown jewels,
Monty was soon very popular
with both staff and tourists.
Even the Royal Family asked
after him when they visited the
Tower. On one memorable
occasion, the alarm system had
just been renewed in the
Wakefield Tower. At the
opening ceremony, the great
doors were opened and the
alarm switched on. An official
was about to cross the threshold
with great solemnity to test the
rays, when suddenly little
Monty, determined to steal the
limelight, trotted ahead of him.
To everyone's consternation no
alarm sounded as the little dog
passed through. It was only
triggered off by the official. To
general hilarity it was then
discovered that the rays didn't
reach the floor. To stop thieves
crawling through on their
stomachs, they were
subsequently readjusted.

Rob, another patrol mongrel who also won a Dickin medal, happily survived to receive it and thoroughly enjoyed being mobbed like a Beatle at the ceremony. A glorious grinning Borderline Collie with a large black patch over one eye, he served with the SAS and took part in landings in North Africa with the infantry unit, and then served with them again in Italy. Most of the work was extremely dangerous. Known as the 'Paradog', he made over twenty parachute landings, and guarded small parties exploring enemy territory. Like Bob, Rob saved numerous lives.

A third Dickin Medal was deservedly won by an Alsatian cross called Brian, who served in the 13th Battalion Airborne Division. Landing in Normandy, he did enough drops to become a qualified parachutist. In his official photograph Brian is shown with his head cocked on one side. Rather like American soldiers in films who always wear their peaked caps at a raffish un-English angle, he exudes a jolly chocolate-boxy charm which would never be seen in a pure breed Alsatian.

RATS — THE DOG SOLDIER
Easily the most famous of postwar mascots, Rats, the jaunty little mongrel, adored soldiers and for many years attached himself to different British army units in Crossmaglen, one of the most threatened Northern Ireland trouble spots.

Serving with the Grenadier Guards, the Marines, the Queen's Own Highlanders and the Welsh Guards, Rats went on ceaseless patrols, car chases and helicopter flights, when he gave everyone heart attacks, leaping thirty feet to the ground, as the helicopter came down to land.

He was shot at more times than anyone could remember; he was blown up by bombs, including a firebomb which burnt several inches off his tail. Four pieces of metal lay trapped along his spine; shotgun pellets still lodged in his chest; he was run over twice by cars in the course of duties, leaving him with permanently bent paws. Worst of all, being such an affectionate dog, he had to suffer the heartbreak of losing a beloved master and finding a new one each time a unit moved.

Gradually his fame spread, and he became not only an IRA hit target, but also a national celebrity, receiving two sacks of mail a day, which took six fulltime soldiers to answer. He was also given numerous presents from admirers, including one old lady who sent him last week's copy of the *Radio Times* and *TV Times* each week.

His greatest service to the army, however, was boosting morale. 'At the head of the patrol, half strutting, half waddling briskly and happily ahead, he gave the illusion that all was right with the world and death and violence merely a bad dream.'

Or as another soldier who served with him said, 'Rats was an oasis of friendship in a desert of sadness.'

Finally in 1980 the exertions of war took their toll on his small frame. On doctor's orders, he was given an honourable retirement, and a very distinguished passing-out parade. Now he lives happily in Kent, where new hobbies include chasing the local pheasants.

BOBBY OF MAIWAND

Bobby, a white mongrel, was attached to the 2nd Battalion, the Royal Berkshire Regiment, with whom he went to India when the Afghan War broke out. He was present at the famous Battle of Maiwand in 1880 when the British were overwhelmed by an enemy ten times their number. His battalion was gradually whittled down, until they were all killed and only Bobby, who'd stood barking defiantly at the head of the gallant little band throughout the engagement, was left. Taken prisoner, he later joined the remnants of the regiment, at Kandahar. Back in England, Bobby, wearing a smart scarlet coat trimmed with fake pearls, was presented to Queen Victoria. She listened to his story with rapt attention, begged to see his back where he'd been wounded, and pinned the Afghan Medal on his collar. After being taken up by royalty, Bobby became very much above himself, and refused to fraternise with any of the local dogs. Nemesis descended in the form of a hansom cab which ran him over in Gosport. Queen Victoria is said to have cried when she heard this sad news.

PRINCE – THE MIRACLE FINDER

Prince, an Irish terrier, was devoted to his master, Private James Brown of the North Staffordshire Regiment, and was quite inconsolable when Mr Brown was posted to France in September 1914. Then one day he disappeared from his home in Hammersmith, and to everyone's amazement turned up at Armentières a few weeks later, and tracked down his master in the trenches in a frenzy of delight. Because no one could believe the story, the Commanding

Victorian values

The Victorians, who rated fidelity and devotion high on their list of virtues, liked the idea of dogs as heroes. Artists like Landseer catered for this in such pictures as *A Distinguished Member of the Humane Society*. There were innumerable books anthropomorphising doggy heroes. Happily, authors like Dickens were able to create dogs like Jip in *David Copperfield* and Bullseye in *Oliver Twist* who were as much personalities as the human characters.

MEDIEVAL DOGS

Throughout medieval Europe hunting remained the passion and the prerogative of the nobility. They kept vast numbers of hounds (whose food the peasants were expected to provide) and vied with each other as to the excellence of their packs and the abundance of game hunted and killed.

The Bayeaux Tapestry, embroidered shortly after the successful Norman invasion of 1066, shows Harold setting off for Normandy with both his hounds and his hawks. No gentleman would think of travelling without the means to indulge in the pleasures of the chase. A number of other tapestries survive from this period, many showing hunting scenes in great detail. The Lady and the Unicorn, a series of six tapestries believed to be Flemish and woven in the fifteenth century, show tiny and decorative dogs. Small greyhounds and little 'shock' dogs, with hindquarters and tails shaved so that they resembled lions, were the pets and playthings of the ladies of the court.

Decorative detail in churches of the period sometimes shows dogs, in a more domestic role. One medieval stained-glass window shows a couple asleep in bed with a small dog curled up on the coverlet. Carvings on misericords and pew ends show shepherds with their sheepdogs, house watchdogs, and dogs as thieves. Effigies on tombs are sometimes accompanied by small dogs lying at the feet of their master. These may be cast in brass or carved from stone and are believed to symbolise fidelity. Perhaps too there was a hope that they might warm the feet of the dead in the way their live relatives warmed the feet of those living in draughty baronial halls.

References to dogs can be found in Chaucer, probably the best known being the 'smale houndes' kept by the prioress who wept bitterly at their death. Their diet of roast flesh, milk and bread made from the finest flour was a great deal better than that of most of the populace of the time.

Officer had master and dog paraded in front of him next morning. Evidently Prince had cunningly attached himself to some troops who were crossing the Channel, and by some sixth sense had managed to locate his master. He became the hero of the regiment, and fought beside his master for the rest of the war.

BRAVERY

One of Fortnum's great loves in Putney is a mongrel virgin, a dog called Emma Ferris. She is not spayed but repeatedly repels all male advances, including those of Fortnum, who has courted her assiduously for six years. She hates it, however, if he pays court to anyone else. One day, perhaps to trigger off some reaction, he brought Gypsy Nightingale, one of his many other girlfriends, to call on her. Emma saw them both off in a frenzy of rage, rather like Elizabeth I giving the Earl of Leicester the elbow for dallying with Amy Robsart.

Finally it is nice to know that the age of chivalry is not quite dead. Even though Emma has spurned Fortnum's paw, he still protects her when she is in trouble. One winter night in 1980 she was going for a late night walk through the churchyard with her master, when suddenly two drunks came out of a nearby pub. Seeing Emma in the street lamp light, and envisaging some sport, they moved in yelling and kicking at her with huge bovver boots. Next minute a brindle fury shot from the shadows, and Fortnum hurled himself on the drunks, sinking his teeth into their legs, barking hysterically, and despatching them howling back to the pub. He then escorted Emma and her master back through the churchyard, walking shoulder to shoulder with Emma, and not leaving her side until she was safely back in her own home.

Our family didn't hear about this heroic exploit for forty-eight hours, but when we did Fortnum was slightly bemused, but delighted, to be decorated with a red bow, and given a whole box of Yorkies (the chocolates, not the Terriers, which he no doubt would have preferred).

SAVIOURS OF CORINTH

The citadel of Corinth was suddenly attacked one night and, while the soldiers slept in peaceful oblivion of what was happening, the town was defended by its fifty courageous watchdogs, all save one fighting to the death. That one survivor ran to the gates of the town and gave the alarm, at which the sleeping soldiers awoke, rose to the defence and the attack was then repulsed. This heroic survivor of the brigade of watchdogs was given a pension and a collar of solid silver which bore the inscription: 'To Soter, defender and saviour of Corinth, placed under the protection of his friends.'

HISTORIC HERO

We are all familiar with the *cave canem* mosaic from the house of the poet in Pompeii, but there is also a memorial stone still to be seen there in the ruins to a dog that saved its child master from water, fire and thieves. Ironically, it was unable to save the little boy from the volcano, Vesuvius, when its engulfing lava destroyed the town.

Opposite:

A damp outlook

Digby was picked up by a kind member of the public, who had found him wandering aimlessly in the rain amongst the heavy London traffic. A short time later he was in a background of barking dogs and mewing cats, signing on to the Lost Legion. A medical, a brush down, and after a thorough cleaning he sat, cosily wrapped in a towel, staring in sheer wonder at the kind treatment he had received. But now he was just a number in a giant book – with any luck his owner might turn up; if they didn't, then his chances were not all that rosy.

Freddie Reed

The Sick, Injured or Elderly Dog

Observe your dog well at feeding times and when he is relieving himself. Your dog will let you know when he is off-colour, but if you have any doubts contact your veterinarian. It is safer (and frequently cheaper) to make this contact at the first sign of trouble.

It is you, however, who are best placed to know if anything is wrong with your dog. If your instinct tells you your dog is ill, you must first discover whether or not he is in pain. Examine him carefully by running your hands over him firmly, searching for tenderness, swelling, excessive heat or shivering. Look at his coat: a dry, staring coat will indicate inferior health. Very cold ears, very hot thighs, a dry, brown or coated tongue, bloodshot or yellow-tinged eyes, bad breath, rapid breathing or wheezing, and especially distress, indicate a sick dog. Having established that there is some form of ill-health, we then need to look for symptoms. Is the dog off his food, walking slowly or painfully, or just not his usual active self? If he has diarrhoea or vomiting, there is certainly something amiss. If either persist, the dog needs veterinary attention as soon as possible. Quite apart from the cause, diarrhoea and/or vomiting will bring dehydration which can be fatal without urgent treatment.

You can also learn a great deal from the expression of your dog. Ill-health can be signalled by a pinched, nervous expression or a look of fear or discomfort. As you care for your dog you will get to know him and become aware of any change in his behaviour.

MEDICINES

You will almost certainly be called upon at some time to administer medicine to your dog, in liquid, powder, tablet or capsule form. If appropriate, most dogs may be persuaded to take medicines mixed in food, though this is not always possible if they are off their food; and the medicine will be wasted if the dog does not finish its meal.

To administer a tablet, place it on the back of the dog's tongue with the head held up, close the mouth firmly and massage the outside of the throat to push the tablet down as the dog swallows. Some dogs are particularly crafty, and can hold the tablet to spit out later, even though they seem to have swallowed.

Perhaps the best way to administer medicine is using a 10ml

Opposite:
The picture of health

154

Bees and wasps

Dogs (especially puppies) are prone to investigating the buzzing of bees and wasps. They may pick up insects and be stung in the mouth or, more dangerously, in the throat, where swelling can cause suffocation. Feet are also frequently stung.

While wasps do not leave their stings in their victims, the bees do, and the stings should be removed if visible with a pair of forceps or tweezers. The area can be swabbed with a solution of bicarbonate of soda (a dessertspoonful in a pint of water). If the swelling is substantial inside the mouth or throat a veterinarian should be called. Some dogs are more affected than others by such stings and symptoms may vary from mild pain and irritation (and often salivation if the mouth has been stung) to weakness and pain spreading through the body, vomiting and fever. The condition and symptoms can worsen over a period of six to forty-eight hours after the sting. Antihistamine drugs are used routinely in treatment.

plastic syringe (available from most chemists or your veterinary surgery). If the medicine is in tablet rather than liquid form, crush the appropriate dose and mix into boiled (and cooled) water. Place the patient on a high table or bench, and take the muzzle firmly in one hand, keeping it closed and tilted slightly upwards. With the other hand holding the syringe, part the dog's lips and insert the plastic nozzle through the gap between the back teeth. Pointing the nozzle towards the throat, expel the liquid gently by slowly depressing the plunger with your thumb, allowing your patient time to swallow as the liquid enters its throat across the back of the tongue. Do not hold the head so far back that the dog cannot swallow, and be sure that the liquid trickles rather than surges down, otherwise the dog may choke. When the syringe is empty lower the dog's nose until almost level and then gently massage the throat. Never use a glass syringe which would be highly dangerous for such an operation. Metal ones are also not to be recommended since the sensation of cold steel passing over the teeth is uncomfortable.

All medicines should always be kept locked away. It is useful to have a 'first-aid box' set aside for this purpose. Useful additional items are: a medicine dropper with spare rubber teats, cotton wool balls, sterile gauze dressings, round-tipped scissors, spare plastic syringe, double-sided surgical tape, acriflavine or other mild antiseptic ointment, worming tablets, pure olive oil, eucalyptus oil (see Grooming), soluble aspirin, Epsom salts, a stainless-steel dish and some clean towelling.

The dropper will be useful for dispensing drops of medicine, or eye drops. Double-sided surgical tape is useful for keeping temporary dressings in place and acriflavine is suitable for wounds, cuts and abrasions. Half-tablets of soluble aspirin (in water) will relieve pain and small doses of Epsom salts, also dissolved in water, act as a mild laxative. Pure olive oil is an alternative laxative (about two teaspoonfuls for the average-sized dog) and can also be added to food occasionally (about half a teaspoonful) to give extra gloss to the dog's coat.

ACCIDENTS

A large number of visits to the veterinarian are the result of accidents – on the road and in the home. Many accidents which befall dogs, and especially puppies, are easily avoided. In the home, for example, harmful solutions such as poisons, cleaning fluids, pesticides, paints, fertilisers etc should be out of a puppy's reach and preferably locked away. Keep your dog out of the kitchen when serving hot foods, opening ovens or dealing with boiling water. Burns and scalds can easily occur to dog or human if the dog gets in the way.

Live electric flex is potentially dangerous for a puppy who enjoys playing with, even chewing, such a mobile 'toy'. Electrocution can easily kill a puppy. In such a situation, turn off the electric current before touching the dog. If this is not possible, try to push the dog away from the electrical contact with a wooden stick or broom, or with a rolled newspaper. Insulate yourself first by standing on rubber, glass, wood, dry cloth or newspaper. The victim will probably be unconscious and suffering from burns, especially around the mouth. If breathing has stopped, administer artificial respiration by placing the dog on its side with its tail end higher than its head. Place one hand over its rib cage and the other over the upper side of the abdomen. Apply heavy pressure with both hands and release in about two seconds. Keep this up rhythmically with a momentary pause between each application of pressure. This may be the only chance the dog has in cases of electrocution, drowning, poisoning or asphyxia resulting from smoke or fumes. Call a veterinarian as soon as you can.

If your dog is burnt or scalded it will also need to be examined urgently by a veterinarian, but there are first-aid steps which you can carry out immediately. Burns, caused generally by dry heat, can also result from contact with some chemicals and even ice. Scalds are caused by wet heat from hot liquid or steam. The effects of both

PETS IN SUMMER

Summer is the season of hot, sunny days, long, light evenings, hours spent in the garden, in the countryside or by the sea. But it is also the season when pets need special care and attention if they are to enjoy themselves as much as their owners. Unfortunately, many pets suffer at this time of year because of their owner's neglect and thoughtlessness.

By observing the following basic rules you can protect your pet against summer's perils!

• Provide fresh clean drinking water for your pet at all times and remember to remove any uneaten food as this will go stale much more quickly in hot weather.

• Make sure you provide adequate ventilation for your pet.

• Check your pet regularly for fleas. They present a particular problem in late summer, often causing great discomfort and irritation. In cases of severe infestation a veterinary surgeon will advise the correct course of treatment.

• Keep an eye on your pet for signs of persistent irritation which may be caused by grass seeds. If they get into your pet's eyes, ears or paws these seeds can cause great pain if not dealt with immediately.

• Check your pet for wounds and sore patches as these will become infected more quickly in hot weather. An unattended wound will attract blow flies and could result in maggot infestation. Flies may also be attracted to any soiled areas in your pet's living quarters, so an efficient cleaning programme is essential during the summer.

• Remember that the tar on roads can melt on very hot days, so check your dog for tar on the paws.

• Provide your pet with a place to shelter from the sun and remember that the sun moves around during the day. Dogs may shelter in the house or in a shed if no dangerous tools or chemicals are stored there, but make sure there is adequate ventilation as a shed can become an oven on a hot day.

• Protect your pet against the perils of discarded tools, weedkillers and other chemicals, poisonous plants and, of course, the elements when they are in the garden. It is nice for your pets to enjoy the freedom of the garden during the summer, but great care is needed to make sure they remain safe.

• Avoid leaving pets unattended in cars (see page 85).

• If, despite all precautions, your pet does seem to be suffering from too much heat and sun DON'T throw cold water over him – the shock may be great enough to kill! Cool water introduced gradually to a victim of heat stroke will help in an emergency but, as with any suspicion of illness and injury, veterinary advice must be sought immediately.

• The PDSA provides free veterinary treatment for those genuinely unable to afford private veterinary fees.

Hold still now . . . what beautiful eyes you've got!

Time on your hands?

When considering whether or not to have a dog, please take into account the amount of time it will be left on its own. More than five hours is really too long. Dogs need company, and, if boredom sets in, the dog will wreck the house for want of something better to do. Also, if the dog has a stomach upset he may be unable to remain clean indoors for a long time – and it distresses a dog dreadfully to be compelled to foul his home. Dogs are extremely clean creatures, as one can see from observing young puppies in the nest. Even though they cannot yet see, once they have control of their bodily functions they will crawl as far as they can from their mother before relieving themselves.

injuries are similar, and both can vary in severity and corresponding tissue damage. A complication is that the dog's fur will often obscure the damage produced by a scald, though a burn can usually be visible from the hair burnt around the site. The skin surface will also be moist and inflamed and the dog could well be in shock.

Burns and scalds must not be contaminated, so cover the area with a sterile, dry, absorbent gauze dressing. Keep the dog warm and give cold water to drink. If the injury is caused by an acid chemical, bathe with a weak solution of sodium bicarbonate; if by such chemicals as caustic soda (alkali) mix equal parts of vinegar and water to irrigate the wound before dressing with sterile gauze. If the dog has been in contact with vehicle oil or any chemical, call a veterinarian and if possible describe the substance over the telephone (from its container). Waste no time, especially if some of the chemical has been consumed.

These accidents can be avoided by keeping all chemicals locked away from the dog. Added precautions include keeping dogs away from bonfires (and particularly fireworks), hotplates, hair-curling equipment and other heated electrical appliances, lighted cigarettes and matches (which present an additional danger if chewed up). Use convector heaters instead of barred electric fires; protect gas and solid-fuel fires with appropriate guards; do not place hot drinks where a dog can upset them and if you use rubber hot-water bottles, cover them heavily with cloth to avoid skin contact. These precautions are doubly important in the presence of an untrained puppy.

Keep children's toys away from puppies. Dogs of all ages should be protected from all small or sharp objects which may prove dangerous playthings. Leftover bones, such as chop or chicken, or aluminium foil which frequently attracts a dog's attention, should be placed where a dog cannot reach them. All house refuse should be out of reach in a secure dustbin.

On the road, a dog should always be on a lead regardless of how well trained you believe it to be. A sudden distraction, such as a cat or a bird, may make a dog run into the road just as a vehicle appears. Training may be forgotten just for that short, lethal second. Even a well trained dog may not respond faultlessly in a dangerous situation, so it is not worth the risk.

To prevent dog fights always bring your dog under control when there is a strange dog around. Bitches in season should not be exercised in public places where they may cause havoc among the male dog population. As a dog owner you must be alert to prevent your dog from causing an accident, or becoming a danger or a nuisance to others.

Broken glass is a particularly nasty and common hazard for dogs, so be on the lookout for it, particularly in urban areas. If your dog is unfortunate enough to be cut, the wound should be bathed in warm salt solution and examined by a veterinarian as soon as possible.

Grass seeds are most certainly hazardous during the summer months for long-eared dogs. Avoid the barley-type of grass with its seeds that can work down into the dog's ear flap causing intense pain. If your dog is unlucky enough to get one of these seeds down his ear, he will shake his head from side to side in varying degrees of distress. Do no try to poke about inside the ear but immediately call a veterinarian.

Frozen ponds and lakes are dangerous, especially if there are ducks about. Your dog may well chase them, following them out onto the thinner ice. If the dog falls into freezing water its chances of survival are small because it cannot climb out; nor can it break the ice around it to reach dry land. If not rescued very quickly it may slip under the ice and drown. Be sure to avoid this hazard: an awareness can save many tragic accidents. Prevention is most certainly the best policy.

Be careful with an old dog's diet – this old fellow needs to lose a few pounds

NURSING A SICK DOG

A dog recovering from illness or surgery is best nursed in its own home and familiar surroundings. You will be the best nurse, with patience, time and love.

A sick dog needs peace and quiet, gentle handling, reassurance, and probably special diet, with nourishing broths, honey and glucose given at regular times. Keep him warm but not uncomfortably hot. Hygiene is very important: hands, feeding bowls, and all equipment should be kept scrupulously clean. A good light is helpful for changing dressings, applying ointments or administering medicines.

Give small, light, fresh, nourishing meals, served moist and warm. A little added fat helps to compensate for the lack of saliva associated with sickness and will also improve palatability. If food is refused totally, a raw egg beaten up in milk and water, with glucose, and a small pinch of salt is often acceptable. This can be administered by syringe when necessary (see Medicines, page 154).

THE ELDERLY DOG

Your canine friend can be considered to be ageing from about ten years old, although dogs do live up to seventeen or, in rare cases, nineteen years. The dog age of ten is roughly equivalent to fifty-six in human years; twelve is equivalent to sixty-six; thirteen to seventy, and a dog of seventeen would be equivalent to a human age of ninety-one.

There is no reason why a dog should not be kept alive as long as it is in good mental and physical health. However, if it is terminally ill or in pain, euthanasia should be considered a final act of kindness.

Diet needs adjustment as age creeps on. Give two, or even three smaller meals rather than one large one. Do not overfeed – less food is needed but it must be of a higher nutritional quality. Obesity can be a problem for older (and younger) dogs. It is perhaps the single greatest danger to a dog's well-being – with exception of cruelty and neglect. In fact, obesity, which affects around 35 per cent of the canine population, is a form of neglect. Some dogs are literally fed to death. Heart, kidneys, respiratory and digestive organs are all strained by excess weight which is the direct cause of many illnesses. It reduces potential lifespan, adds to bone and skeleton complications and reduces the dog's resistance to infection.

To avoid obesity in later life, make sure your dog has a good balanced diet throughout life and as much exercise as he needs. If your dog seems to be putting on excess weight, take steps quickly, before it becomes serious.

Aged dogs run a higher risk of obesity because their dietary needs change in later years and they take less exercise. In general terms, they need less carbohydrate and more protein. The digestive system becomes more sluggish as dogs become older, so their favourite foods should be fed as often as possible – provided, of course, they are appropriate and nutritional ! Honey, egg custard, small quantities of milk, and a vitamin supplement recommended by your veterinarian make useful additives. Small doses of fresh cod-liver oil (an occasional

---

The veterinarian knows best

A healthy dog is also a happy dog, and regular visits to your veterinarian will help to ensure that your puppy grows into a fit and healthy adult.

You should arrange for your puppy to have a check up annually. Your veterinarian will provide you with advice on general health care as well as important things such as annual booster vaccinations and worming, all of which are part of responsible dog ownership.

Remember always to consult your veterinarian or his trained nursing staff if you are in any doubt about your dog's well being.

teaspoonful in the food) help to keep out the winter cold, which affects elderly dogs. An extra blanket in the dog basket may be needed in the depths of winter, and thorough drying is doubly essential after a wet walk. Damp conditions exacerbate arthritis which affects many elderly dogs, so special care will be needed during grooming sessions.

Elderly skin and joints are more sensitive than in earlier years. Teeth should be checked regularly and scaled when necessary. Your veterinarian will advise on possible extraction if any are painful or bad.

Exercise should still be regular but the dog should be allowed to exercise at its own pace with 'special interest' walks to keep it alert.

Make allowances for deafness and impaired eyesight, if they occur, especially with safety and comfort in mind.

Occasionally, aged dogs suffer from periodic incontinence. They are unable to manage for long periods of time without a visit to the garden. A few old newspapers placed near the door at night will help the dog to adjust and to feel less miserable about its failures. Keep the aged dog happy by reassurance and care. Adjust to the changes in his life and help to compensate for them. Above all, keep the aged dog interested as well as happy. Make him feel wanted, as he has always been. Give him regular veterinary checks and extra kindness. By so doing you will help to prolong his life and keep him in good shape mentally and physically through the twilight of his life.

Royal concern

Pepys complains in his diaries that Charles II was more preoccupied with his toy spaniels than the affairs of state. British royalty have always shown a keen interest in dogs and royal portraits often showed the current favourites. Van Dyck's painting of Charles I's children shows mastiffs and toy spaniels as part of the family group.

The good condition and lively expressions of these three handsome Maremmas belie their advancing years

Photographing Dogs

Perhaps you have tried to photograph your dog, many times. The dog would not keep still. You crouched down to be on his level only to find him rushing up at full tilt to enquire the nature of this latest game, sending you flying into an undignified heap on the ground.

Then you tried the action shots! Dog galloped into frame from left, out of frame on the right and out of sight entirely, so quickly that you forgot to fire the shutter. The catalogue of frustration and disaster is endless; heads and feet cut off, blurred subjects, too light or too dark.

So do not despair. Photographing dogs can be great fun and is not really too difficult. On the following pages there are a few professional hints and tips developed over many years of experience and trial and error. They should enable you to capture your dog successfully on film, however much he hates being photographed.

CHOOSING A CAMERA

For the absolute beginner a simple automated camera is a must. Pentax, Nikon and Minolta all have excellent examples which wind the film on, adjust the exposure and even have an automatic zoom lens. You simply place the film in the back, fire the shutter and the film is wound on ready to take pictures. (Film speed is usually limited to ISO 100.) For the more ambitious, there are many extraordinary cameras, some with automatic focussing etc.

Always go to a reputable dealer who will discuss your needs and give advice. It is risky to answer ads in the newspapers or magazines if you do not have specialist knowledge. There are of course excellent second-hand cameras available, usually unwanted gifts or where people have given up photography. Most towns have a shop which deals in second-hand cameras, often with well informed and helpful staff. A new camera carries a year's guarantee, whereas a second-hand one will probably have a three months' guarantee.

ZOOM LENSES

The standard lens for reasonable close-ups is the 50mm, but with this you will have to walk up close to your subject, and the dog may object. A zoom lens enables you to photograph the dog from some distance away according to the range of the lens. It is not necessary

---

Moving house

When you move house your dog will not understand all the strange people tramping around in his master's home and 'stealing' things. On the day of the move leave your dog with a friend or put him in local boarding kennels. When you take him to your new home, shut him somewhere safe, with a bowl of water, his own bed, and something to chew. Go and talk to him as often as you can and, if possible, leave something of your own, with your scent on it, with him. Do not let him out, except on a lead. Above all, in the chaos of moving in, don't forget him. And don't forget to change the address on his collar, too!

to buy the lens made by the manufacturer of your camera, as some specialist manufacturers such as Vivitar and Tamron make superb lenses to fit all models, at a considerably reduced price.

The longer the lens, the slower the exposure, which necessitates a faster film speed in dull weather conditions.

Once you have mastered the zoom lens, it will bring amazing possibilities within reach.

These English Setter pups are certainly enjoying the photo session

FILM TYPES AND USES

There are three types of film; monochrome (black and white), colour transparency and colour negative. The transparency is for slide projection and the colour negative for prints. All are different in their application and their speeds range from ISO 50 to ISO 3200.

For prints, use a ISO 100 film in summer and ISO 200 in the winter. Kodak and Fuji have a remarkable film that self adjusts in indoor lighting to produce correctly balanced results.

The fast ISO 400 (and upwards) is needed to capture dogs on the move.

PLAY SAFE

Buy toys for your dog from a pet shop which should only sell those that are 'safe'. Most dogs love squeaky toys, but they are easily chewed and swallowed. Some dogs disembowel them and eat the 'squeaker'. Give your puppy lots of hard toys to play with – a hard rubber quoit is a great favourite, also a large rubber ball. A large ring made of hard nylon makes an excellent teething ring. Never let your puppy get hold of anything he could swallow, which might cause a blockage. Be wary of electric cables, telephone wires, machines which your puppy could get caught in, or ovens, refrigerators and freezers in which he could get trapped.

Always let sleeping dogs lie. Don't maul your dog about when he's asleep. It is not very sensible to give a puppy a shoe to play with as he cannot discriminate between his old shoe and your new ones.

Throwing sticks for a dog can be a problem, too, because if they are caught awkwardly they can get stuck in his throat. Sticks are best used for throwing into water, at lakes and the seaside. It is also possible to buy a square rubber quoit that floats. If your dog does swim in the sea. 'rinse' him in fresh water before you dry him, to avoid a skin reaction to the sea-water. (Dogs that have dense waterproof undercoats are unlikely to suffer this problem.)

Do not play energetic games with your dog in the midday heat of a summer's day. If he wants to rest somewhere cool, leave him to do just that.

Beware of anglers. They have all sorts of boxes filled with tempting things for a dog, and fish-hooks which seem to be made to catch in any part of the anatomy. If your dog does get a fish-hook in itself, cut off the barbed end, simply remove it and watch for infection.

When there is snow on the ground, check your dog's feet. Lumps of snow can get between toes and pads and be very painful. Once you have de-iced, dry the feet carefully. Applying vaseline before and after is helpful.

When dogs come in from the rain, ensure that feet, chest and abdomen are dry before you let them go to their bed or lie down. Heavy-coated breeds have undercoats which rain does not penetrate, and a damp chamois will dry the coat. If your dog does not mind, use a hair drier. Always ensure that the dog has a dry, warm bed to come home to.

Many people have problems teaching their dog to give up toys/objects. It is a vital lesson and not difficult if you follow these steps. Give your puppy a marrow bone, which will be larger than the puppy's mouth and, therefore, easy to hold. Let the puppy gnaw contentedly for a while, then, with a dog biscuit handy, get down on your hands and knees and say 'Dead' or 'Drop', or whatever command you intend to use. The puppy will not recognise the command and will probably continue to chew the bone. Say 'Dead' again, and put one hand on the bone. Now one of two things will happen. Either the puppy will let you take the bone or he will hang on hard. If he lets you take it, say 'Good dog' and give him the biscuit. Pretend to examine the bone and then give it back to him, saying 'Good dog' again. Such a puppy is no problem, because he will have the confidence that you will always give his precious things back to him. But with the puppy that hangs on to the bone, and may even growl, say 'Dead' again, still holding the bone. Then, with your other hand, open his jaws to release the bone. Say 'Good dog' and give it back to him. Carry on like this until he lets you take the bone, then praise him and give him the biscuit – you're winning.

Always remember to keep commands to one or two syllables. It's no good saying, for instance, 'Now be a good dog and let mistress have that lovely bone.' He will not recognise anything except 'Good dog'. As the puppy grows up, he will come to understand the greater part of what you say, and the sounds he cannot recognise will probably be in tones he can understand, so he will get the general idea, but start off with good clear commands.

Maggers and his owner play silly games. She says 'Doing?', and he starts sorting through his toys. Then he brings a rubber ball to play 'retrieve the ball' in the garden or 'hunt the ball' around the house. And he will sit while his owner leaves the room, closing the door behind her, to hide the ball somewhere else in the house. He has become so good at this that she has run out of hiding places. When they first played this game she would say 'cold', 'warm' or 'warmer', as appropriate, and he soon understood this as well.

Never underestimate your dog. Give him a varied, interesting life, with lots of love, and you will be pleasantly surprised.

BE PREPARED

Make sure that your camera is fully loaded and that you are prepared to meet the challenge. This is no easy foe that you are about to meet, but one that is cunning and able to recognise that he or she is about to be photographed. As you approach, the subject in question may well roll on its back to be stroked, instead of staying in the perfect pose under the soft light of a shady tree. In this situation, walk casually away, and ignore the dog until he returns to that attractive pose. Then turn slowly, camera out of sight until the last moment, and quickly take the picture.

Get your dog used to the camera – especially the flash, to avoid a startled look. Let him see you using the camera often (a pointed object is often seen as a threat). When he has posed well give a reward, a cuddle or a stroke. You will be surprised how quickly your dog becomes a willing and enjoyable subject for your pictures. Do not ever lose your patience and get annoyed, as this will communicate itself quickly to the dog.

You are much more likely to take a successful close-up with a zoom lens

OUTDOOR PHOTOGRAPHY

Outdoor photography really is the most exciting way to capture your dog on film. Its realism surpasses all the indoor effects. For instance, you could photograph your dog in long grass, sitting in a leafy glade, astride an old log, shaking itself after swimming, leaping over obstacles, or fast asleep in half sunlight. Make a mental note of his favourite places and be on the look-out for photographic opportunities on your regular walks, family picnics etc.

The best light for outdoor photography is cloudy-bright. Direct sunlight is too harsh, with dark shadows which burn out coat detail.

Once you have selected the site and the subject is suitably relaxed, get down on your knees (or even stomach) and frame the dog carefully in the viewfinder. Fill the frame, leaving only a small border – do not have a tiny picture in a giant canvas. (If you have only an instamatic with no zoom lens, this is more difficult because you will have to go in closer.) Squeeze the release button on the camera very gently and hold your breath for a moment. Take two or three shots but do not waste film.

All the personality of the Finnish Spitz, captured in natural pose and perfect dappled light

The instamatic viewfinder is a little above the subject so experiment to achieve the right results. Do not let a little rain deter you – a spring or summer's day in the rain can be superb, as most dogs are not worried by anything less than a downpour. Snow is superb but needs care as you will have to go onto manual.

People and dogs together outdoors can make superb pictures, as long as they appear unposed. Spaniels lend themselves particularly to being photographed with children – the trick is to catch the children in a natural, unconcerned pose. Several dogs together can be effective if the picture reflects their different personalities and interaction. Large dogs add a touch of opulence to a human group.

ACTION SHOTS

Capturing your dog in action is a great thrill, especially with the more agile or longhaired breeds, eg, Afghan Hound or Irish Setter. Action photography requires a certain amount of practice if one is to become proficient.

A 'fast' film is required – ISO 400-3200. The very fast film, ISO 3200, can be used under very low light conditions, but it may be somewhat 'grainey'.

It is more difficult to focus on a dog coming towards the camera at speed than on one moving across one's line of vision. In the latter case, you can keep the dog in focus by moving the camera with the dog, firing the shutter at the most effective moment. This technique is known as panning. Practise this action as often as you can, even without film in the camera, keeping your motion as smooth as possible.

If you can get two people to help, by sending the dog from one to another, this will be a great boon. Take note of the position of the sun when organising your helpers and the path the dog will follow. The general rule is, as for other outdoor work; have the sun behind the camera, except for special effects. It is sometimes possible to have the sun behind the subject giving a 'halo' effect, although remember not to have the light shining directly into the lens.

For the last word in action shots you will need a motor drive on the camera. With this you can take repeated exposures, giving the whole series of movement.

INDOOR PHOTOGRAPHY

There are two ways of photographing indoors: flash or available (natural) light. The latter is preferable if you can get an exposure of not less than a thirtieth of a second. Below that, it is extremely difficult to get a sharp exposure unless one is very experienced and the subject is still.

For the flash user, the main problem is 'red eye', when the retina of the eye reflects and causes this strange effect. To avoid this, do not aim the flash into the dog's eyes; bounce it off a white reflector or wall. This will decrease the exposure speed of the film; experiment to produce good results.

Bright natural light will often produce shadows on one side of the

---

A gift remembered

Dita the Dalmatian dearly loved a friend who had given her a hard rubber ball when she was just a puppy. When told 'Phyllis is coming to tea', she would fetch the right ball and sit with it, ready to give it to Phyllis. She was never taught to do this. Dogs are far more intelligent than we suspect.

Time to go

Kate had some good ideas. When she thought a visitor had oustayed her welcome, she would bring in the lady's hat, or get up on the chair behind her and squeeze her off it.

The elegance of an Irish Setter in motion

dog, but this can be delightful. (Do not try to add light with tungsten bulbs, as this will give a yellowed effect.) For example, a dog is lying in a shaft of sunlight, the light gently falling across his head and shoulder, the rest of his body in gentle shadow. Using flash it would even the lighting and ruin the 'mood'. For these pictures, use Fujicolor 400 or Kodacolor 400 films.

If you do use flash, do not approach too closely or the light will burn out the subject. This applies especially to instamatic cameras with a pop-up flash.

BACKGROUNDS AND SETTINGS

Colours reflect their own spectrum and so a green material gives a green cast and a red one a red cast etc. This is not visible to the naked eye but sensitive photographic film picks up all colours. A white dog seated on a red cushion or chair would come out with a red cast; a brown dog would appear darker etc. 'Cool' colours such as blue and green are safer. Study the colours which suit your particular breed. If you want to create an attractive setting with a bowl of flowers, etc, be careful not to distract attention from the dog.

Always avoid fussy backgrounds such as floral patterned fabrics or wallpaper.

BLACK AND WHITE PHOTOGRAPHY

Black and white photography suits dogs admirably – the dramatic quality is greater than in colour, and textures come out much better. If you have a SLR camera you can even use the very fast film and capture dogs on the run much more effectively. Also, black and white gives you the opportunity to start your own developing – though you should avoid too much contrast to prevent 'burn-out'.

The Beauty Contest

Let us assume that you decide you would like to show your pedigree dog. The first step is to check up on what your dog is supposed to look like. A good idea is to go back to the breeder and ask for an honest opinion. The breeder will go over the dog, as the judge will do in the show ring, explaining the salient points and commenting upon how perhaps some could be improved, perhaps comparing these with one of the breeder's dogs.

A dog show is merely a beauty contest, so you will not win awards with a dog that has a fault (eg an undershot jaw), or with one that is not entire ie, spayed bitches (except for life saving reasons), castrated dogs, or dogs with undescended testicles. In your breed's Club Yearbook you will find the breed standard to which your dog should conform. This is also available from the Kennel Club. Here again, the person who bred your dog will be able to explain it all to you. If you bought your dog for working (Field Trials, Obedience, etc) there are different considerations.

If the breeder tells you that it would be worthwhile entering your dog for shows, put yourself in his or her hands and ask how it is best to start. In the show ring itself your dog must stand four-square and alert (unless it is a German Shepherd). The judge will then 'go over' the dog, examine its bite and ask you both to 'move', probably by describing a triangle. This is easier than it sounds. All you have to do is leave the judge, with your dog on your left, and head towards an imaginary point on the far right-hand corner. When you reach that point, make a sharp left turn of some 45 degrees and head towards another imaginary point. Then make another sharp left turn and head back towards the judge. Stop a few feet in front of him and make your dog stand alert again. By now the judge will have looked closely at your dog and seen it move from behind, from across and from in front, to identify any gait problems.

Remember, when leaving the show ring, PRAISE your dog. After all, whatever the result, he's done his best for you.

Before going to a show it is advisable to attend a few ringcraft classes, where your dog will become used to being handled, to trotting around in circles and triangles and to standing quietly. It will also give you a chance to learn how to show your dog.

Opposite:
Merely a beauty contest!

Opposite:
Close encounter at Crufts

If you have a long-coated breed you may well need to do some trimming prior to a show. Your breeder should be able to advise on this. If you have a Standard Poodle, on the other hand, you will need to have it prepared by a professional. This probably applies to some of the terrier breeds as well. There are professional handlers, too, but hopefully you are going to show your dog yourself, just for the fun and enjoyment of doing so.

Entries for shows have to be in six to eight weeks in advance, and often earlier for championship shows. The publications *Our Dogs* and *Dog World* list all the details about shows and where to get the relevant schedules. Make sure your dog is transferred to your ownership at the Kennel Club. Another tip: do not enter every class in the hope that then you must surely get noticed and placed in one of them. Read the class definitions carefully before deciding which to enter. If it is a Breed Club Open or Championship Show there will be many classes and a judge who specialises in your breed. Then there are shows that are open to all breeds, at which there may be only one or two classes for your breed, or perhaps none at all, so you will have to enter variety classes, and probably have an 'all rounder' judge.

You will need a safety pin or ring card clip, so that your ring number can be displayed on you, not the dog. As dogs are not shown with collars, a slip lead is also required. There are often stands at shows where you can buy everything a dog could want.

You learn a lot from sitting at the ringside as a spectator, watching others. Entrants at Championship Shows come from anywhere in the British Isles – all chasing Junior Warrants or Challenge Certificates, so there is always a high standard of breed quality and often enormous classes of forty to fifty dogs.

Mongrels get their chance to show off in the agility competitions

CRUFTS

Charles Cruft, founder of the world's premier dog show, was a born showman. Son of a jeweller, he was a travelling salesman for James Spratt who had just begun manufacturing 'dog cakes'. The business took Charles to the Continent and on one of these visits he was asked to organise a 'Canine Exhibition' in Paris. The show was a great success and he was asked to repeat the exercise in Britain. Putting his considerable flair for publicity to good use (and making a considerable profit into the bargain) he began to organise the series of dog shows that still bear his name. He introduced many new breeds at the old Agricultural Hall in Islington where the show was held.

In those days, if a show ran for two days your

CRUFTS BEST IN SHOW

1977 English Setter Ch. Bournehouse Dancing Master

1978 Fox Terrier (Wire) Ch. Harrowhill Huntsman

1979 Kerry Blue Terrier Ch. Callaghan of Leander

1980 Retriever (Flat-coated) Ch. Shargleam Blackcap

1981 Irish Setter Ch. Astley's Portia of Rua

1982 Poodle (Toy) Ch. Grayco Hazlenut

1983 Afghan Hound Ch. Montravia Kaskarak Hitari

1984 Lhasa Apso Ch. Saxonsprings Hackensack

1985 Poodle (Standard) Ch. Montravia Tommy-Gun

1986 Airedale Terrier Ch. Gunger Xmas Carol

1987 Afghan Hound Ch. Viscount Grant

1988 English Setter Show Ch. Starlite Express at Valsett

1989 Bearded Collie Ch. Potterdale Classic of Moonhill

Right: *Every inch a winner – Supreme Champion Crufts 1989, the Bearded Collie Ch. Potterdale Classic of Moonhill*

dog had to be there for two days and many dogs were sent to shows by rail. The boxes were collected by agents of the show management who benched, fed, watered and sometimes showed them.

Charles Cruft died in 1938, two years after the Jubilee show. His wife ran one further show in 1939 and then in 1942 she passed the show over to the Kennel Club, which ran its first Cruft's in 1948 at Olympia. Cruft's is a 'different' dog show, as a dog must qualify at another Championship Show to be eligible. With around 10,000 entries and vast numbers of spectators, there is an air of excitement not experienced at any other show – and a win at Crufts is among the top honours.

Mistress and dog in close harmony during an obedience competition

Best in Show

DOG SHOWS

No dog show may be held without first obtaining permission from the Kennel Club and paying the appropriate fee. Each type of show is subject to a set of comprehensive rules and regulations laid down by the Kennel Club as well as its own rules laid down by the committee organising the show. They cover everything from what should be included in the schedule to the circumstances in which a late comer to the show may be entered in another class. The following is a brief summary only of each type of show.

EXEMPTION SHOWS

Exemption shows cannot be run by registered canine societies. As the name implies, they are 'exempt' from Kennel Club rules and regulations, except for the simple set of rules to prevent them competing with shows licensed by the Kennel Club.

An exemption show can have up to four pedigree classes and any number of 'novelty' classes. Cross-bred dogs can be entered in novelty classes. Exemption shows are often held to raise money for charity and many exhibitors use them to help their dogs become accustomed to the show ring, so the quality of some of the exhibits is often higher than you would expect. They are also fun! The classes are usually well filled, so, if you lose your disappointment is shared by all the others, and if you win it is a considerable achievement. Some exhibitors show almost entirely at Exemption Shows. They prefer the atmosphere and enjoy the day out.

Such shows are easy to organise and almost always make a reasonable profit. Prizes can usually be begged from local firms in the name of the organisation or charity running the show and the only expenses are the Kennel Club Licence, ring numbers, rosettes, advertising in the canine press and local papers, prize cards, insurance and a present for the judge. Entries are usually taken 'on the day' during the two hours or so before judging begins.

MATCHES

Matches are usually organised between competing teams representing breed or general canine societies. Only registered canine societies are allowed to run or take part in Matches and a Kennel Club Licence is required. Apart from the licence, a judge, ring numbers and a rosette or prize for the winner, very little organisation is required.

As exhibitors enter their dogs on the day with the Secretary or Show Manager, they are placed in two lists, according to the team they represent, until they are all entered. Two numbers are drawn out of a hat, one from each team, and the dogs are judged. The winner goes forward into the next round as in a knockout tournament, the one remaining at the end being the winner.

Societies will often run two Matches during an evening – one for puppies, perhaps, and one for adult dogs.

PRIMARY SHOWS

These shows allow societies to hold a very limited number of classes without going to the expense of printing a schedule, receiving entries and printing a catalogue in advance. Exhibitors may enter on the

THE EARLIEST DOG SHOWS

The first recognised association for dog owners appears to have been founded in 1776, but there do not appear to have been competitive beauty shows until well into the next century. During that period 'exhibitions' were held where dogs were displayed, bought and sold and where other forms of 'sporting competitions' were held. These would have included bear and badger baiting, dog fights and, very popular, ratting competitions. Despite the law of 1835 banning such sports, in 1884 an English Toy Terrier called Tiny the Wonder was winning bets for his owner, one Jeremy Shaw, a London publican, by killing up to two hundred rats in less than one hour!

By this time, dog shows or 'bad' matches were being organised and credit for the first breed show proper must go to the Pug fraternity for 'A Great Exhibition of the Pugs of all Nations' which was held on 30 May 1850. It was really a charity event which actually made a story for *The Illustrated London News*.

The first organised dog show where 'official' judging took place was in Newcastle-upon-Tyne in 1859. It was confined to Pointers and Setters and three judges were appointed to each breed. Despite this effort at fair play, one of the Setter judges owned the winning Pointer and one of the Pointer judges

day, as with Matches.

Like a Match, a Primary Show is an enjoyable social which provides exhibitors with the opportunity to give their dogs practice as well as providing a training ground for judges.

SANCTION SHOWS

These are the first of the Kennel Club's Licenced Shows. A schedule of rules, classes and judges must be published (and sent to the Kennel Club), entries must be received in advance, and a catalogue printed (including names, owners, breeders and breeding of each dog, a list of the classes and the dogs entered in each class).

The number of classes is restricted as are the times at which they may be held. Exhibitors must be members of the society holding the show. They remain small, friendly events, for local exhibitors.

LIMITED SHOWS

As with Sanction Shows, exhibitors must be members of the club running the event, but Limited Shows have less restrictions on the number of classes and the show may be held at any time. Although most Limited Shows are quite small, a few have considerable prestige. Some of our major canine societies hold limited shows for their members only and the competition at these events can be very hot.

OPEN SHOWS

Open Shows are open to all exhibitors and any Kennel Club registered dog. Open shows can be of any size so long as the Kennel Club considers that adequate facilities are available. Breed associations and general canine societies may hold them, and they range from as few as ten to over a thousand classes.

At some shows the dogs are benched – always at the larger Championship Shows. Benches are partitioned ranks of low stalls on which dogs can be placed for the duration of the show (except, of course, when they are being judged).

The Open Show is generally regarded as a more serious stage of competition than the other licensed shows, but it has suffered a decline as exhibitors have become increasingly able (or prepared) to travel further afield to Championship Shows.

CHAMPIONSHIP SHOWS

Each year the Kennel Club fixes the number of Challenge Certificates which will be available for each breed two years hence. The figure is arrived at through a formula which takes into account the number of dogs being shown during the previous two years. So, the more dogs being shown in a given breed, the more sets of Challenge Certificates will be available in two years' time (except in the very largest breeds). A dog has to beat all of the others of its sex at a show to gain one and then has to gain two more under different judges to become a Champion. CCs or 'tickets' are very difficult to come by, and it is probably harder to make up a Champion in the United Kingdom than in any other country in the world.

The general Championship Shows number their entries in thousands and most are held over two, three, four and even five days and, of course, running such a show is almost a full-time job. Some general Championship Shows (and many Open Shows) are run by agricultural societies or local town or city authorities. Nevertheless, although they are largely independent of the show and society structure of the Kennel Club, they must still agree to be bound by the Kennel Club rules.

owned the winning Setter! The following year the Birmingham Dog Show Society held the first Exhibition for all breeds. At this time there were no catalogues or any form of registration of dogs, so each breed was entered in its own kennel name in the equivalent of the one Open class allowed for each breed.

By 1873, showing dogs had become a popular pastime and something had to be done to try to sort out the problems which arose from so many dogs having the same name, and various other common 'unscrupulous practices'.

At this time the Member of Parliament for Ettringham was S.E. Shirley who had run an efficient and successful show at the Crystal Palace in 1872. It

was decided to form a Kennel Club to legislate on canine matters relating to dog shows and to publish a Stud Book – with Shirley as its first Chairman, and subsequently President. By 1904 – a remarkably short time bearing in mind that attempts to organise other, rival national Kennel Clubs had been made – The Kennel Club had established itself as the ruling authority. This was achieved despite the fact that there were less than 300 members, until very recently.

In the 110 years since its formation, the Kennel Club has grown so that it now handles around 200,000 registrations each year plus all the work concerned with the regulation of over 4,200 dog shows annually. The Kennel Club's aims and objectives have been copied the world over.

THE KENNEL CLUB

The Kennel Club was founded in 1873 just over twenty years after the first formally recorded dog show which was held in Newcastle on Tyne in June 1859. By 1900 agreement had been reached with other aspiring societies and nearly thirty Championship Shows were being held each year. The Kennel Club was very much a gentleman's club at that time and only men were entitled to be members – a regime which lasted until 1978, although a Ladies Branch was founded early this century. Membership is still very restricted, the maximum number allowed by the rules being seven hundred and fifty.

PUBLICATIONS

Kennel Club publications include the breed standards, the set of Kennel Club Yearbooks, which list general and breed canine societies, Kennel Club Rules and Regulations and lists of members and associate members. The output has been increased enormously recently by the introduction of new publications such as the Rescue Directory, lists of affixes, the Canine Code and the list of Championship Show judges. The major publication is the monthly journal, The Kennel Gazette, which contains articles of general interest, as well as official notifications. These include the full list of shows which have been authorised (with the exception of Exemption Shows), Kennel Club official announcements, changes in the rules, regulations or breed standards, publications of requested affixes, judges for shows which have Championship status, lists of dogs which have passed the various breed certificate schemes and application of membership or associateship of the Kennel Club.

A supplement compiled by the registration

Colour confusion

The identification of retrievers by colour causes a great deal of confusion. The Kennel Club, in its wisdom, classifies all Chesapeake Bay, Curly Coated, Flat Coated, Golden and Labrador as 'Retriever', with, for example, the word 'Labrador' in brackets afterwards. A Labrador-Retriever (Labrador) may be black, liver or *yellow*, never *golden*. A Golden-Retriever (Golden) is always *golden*, never *yellow*.

Relaxing after a hard day at the show

department, giving details of all puppies registered at the Kennel Club, and changes of name and owners of registered dogs.

AWARDS

The awards department keeps a record of each dog, including details of its performance at major shows. The complete record of wins, parentage and ownership is published in the Stud Book, which has been published every year since the Kennel Club's inception.

The establishment of a computer section at The Kennel Club has greatly increased the capacity and accuracy of records. The database already provides much important material and should certainly improve the breeding of pedigree dogs in the future by making relevant statistical information available.

SHOWS

The show department collates applications for shows, publishes the show calendar, keeps show records, organises the checking of schedules and entry forms, allocates Challenge Certificates to shows and does the work associated with checking the qualifications of judges. The Crufts department is the smallest at the Kennel Club, but it works full time, all the year round for the big event at Earls Court in early February. The Kennel Club registers 200,000 dogs each year, and, although its prime objects are related to the interests of pure-bred dogs, much work is now done to represent the interests of the world of dogs as a whole.

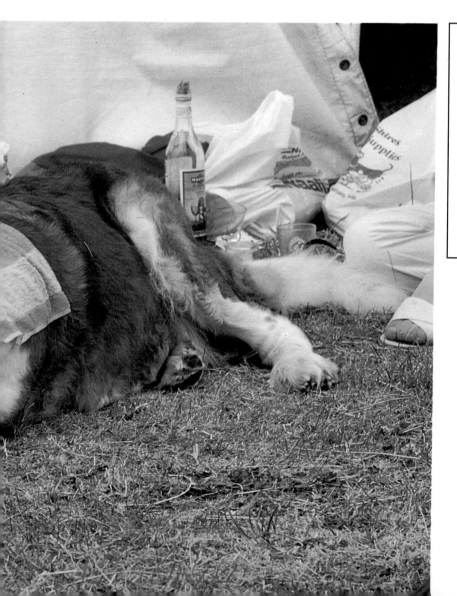

TOP TEN BREED REGISTRATIONS, 1987

1 German Shepherd Dog (Alsatian) -17,000 registered
2 Retriever (Labrador)
3 Retriever (Golden)
4 Yorkshire Terrier
5 Cavalier King Charles Spaniel
6 Rottweiler
7 Spaniel (Cocker)
8 Dobermann
9 Staffordshire Bull Terrier
10 Spaniel (English Springer)

Choosing a Boarding Kennel

Many people like to take their dogs away with them but your dog may not travel well, your holiday accommodation may not take pets and there may be local bye-laws prohibiting dogs from beaches and parks. Such restrictions may tempt you to leave your dog in the car, but there is too much danger of the dog overheating, even on a mild day, for this ever to be safe.

Of course if you are going abroad your dog will not be able to go

Quarantine kennels

with you, unless you want him to spend six months in quarantine on your return. Do not even contemplate taking your dog on a boating holiday if you are planning to put into a continental port. On your return that might also mean a quarantine period for your dog even if it did not go ashore!

Leaving your dog with friends or relatives also has drawbacks. Do they really understand dogs? Is their garden escape proof? Do they have boisterous children who leave doors and gates open? Could they cope if your dog became unwell? Do they have pets of their own which might resent a canine intruder?

The answer is to give your dog its own holiday in the safe keeping of a licensed boarding kennel. This should be pre-planned, as is your own holiday, and not a last-minute decision.

CHOOSING THE RIGHT KENNELS

Perhaps friends or acquaintances can recommend a kennel they have found satisfactory. You may find notices in your veterinarian's surgery and there are sure to be several listings under 'Boarding Kennels' in the *Yellow Pages*. Make a list of possible kennels, then (recommended or not) make an appointment to visit the premises. You should, of course, have the attention of the proprietor, or manager, not just a quick tour of the premises with a kennel attendant. You will need to discuss your dog's idiosyncrasies or any health problems.

What should you look for in a boarding kennel? If you have never been to a boarding kennel before, do not be disturbed by the noisy welcome. Dogs are supposed to be lively and interested in what is going on. If a vocal canine greeting is not evident and the boarders do not look fit and frisky there is something wrong.

Ask which kennel your dog would occupy if you made a firm booking. Is it big enough? All kennels should be at least average room height. They should not be 'hutches' – not even for small dogs. Ideally, each kennel should lead into its own outside run via a hatch which is large enough for your dog to negotiate easily. Check that the dog will also be given other exercise daily. This may be free play in a securely fenced compound, or in some cases a lead walk on the kennel property.

In boarding kennels which do not have attached outside runs to each compartment, the dogs should be taken individually to an outside free play area several times each day. Check the type of facilities being offered by any kennel you inspect and the amount of individual outdoor exercise arranged for each boarder at the height of the busy boarding season. Is it enough? Of course dogs from the same household may be kennelled together or may play together in the exercise compound, but they should not be kennelled with, or put out to play unsupervised with, dogs belonging to other people.

The kennels should be insured to cover any veterinary attention. At good kennels this is included in the boarding fees. Do not expect to board a puppy as it will be much more vulnerable, and it is best not to take very old dogs to boarding kennels if they have never

Dog. *n.*

A kind of additional or subsidiary Deity designed to catch the overflow and surplus of the worship. The Divine Being in some of his smaller and silkier incarnations takes, in the affection of Woman, the place to which there is no human male aspirant. The Dog is a survival – an anachronism. He toils not, neither does he spin, yet Solomon in all his glory never lay upon a door-mat all day long, sun-soaked and fly-fed and fat, while his master worked for the means wherewith to purchase an idle wag of the Solomonic tail, seasoned with a look of tolerant recognition.

Ambrose Bierce,
The Devil's Dictionary

Comfort before all else

The Pekinese
Adore their ease
And slumber like the dead;
In comfort curled
They view the world
As one unending bed.

E.V.Lucas

Left:
Portrait of a Pyrenean
and right:
At the other end of the scale –
finishing touches for a Pomeranian

Below:
A lesson in camouflage from a
Gordon Setter

experienced that sort of environment before. Most boarding kennels would not take bookings for puppies, or aged and infirm dogs.

Before they accept a dog all licensed boarding kennels will require an up-to-date certificate of immunisation against distemper, hardpad, leptospirosis and canine parvovirus. There may be other conditions such as immunisation against kennel cough. Kennels should be generally tidy, without any strong odours. A little shabbiness is not necessarily a sign of negligence, but totally ramshackle buildings, a general lack of cleanliness and a very strong odour of disinfectant are things to watch out for. Boarding kennels do not need to reek of disinfectant, as the best disinfecting products do not have overpoweringly strong odours. Strong disinfectant smells may be present to mask other odours. They can also affect your dog's eyes and paws.

Drinking water should be available at all times. The bowls should be clean and the water fresh. Are there dirty food dishes lying about? Are there half-eaten meals? Ask what sort of food is given to the

---

Fooling around

The great pleasure of a dog is that you may make a fool of yourself with him and not only will he not scold you but he will make a fool of himself too.

Samuel Butler

PETS FOR THERAPY

STUDYING ANIMALS AS PETS

The subject of human-pet relationships has recently become the focus of serious scientific study. In the last twelve years, important conferences have been held in this country, the USA and Austria to investigate the human-pet relationship. This subject has proved to be of interest to scientists in various different fields including veterinary surgeons, biologists, human behaviourists, specialists in paediatric and geriatric medicine, psychologists, general practitioners and social workers. Folklore has long recognised the value that pets have as a natural therapeutic aid for certain conditions and certain types of person. These scientific studies are confirming that pets make life more interesting for some people and act as a psychological aid for people who are deeply withdrawn.

The subject is very wide and is now beginning to benefit from continuous research but there are two particular areas where pets can be proved to have special advantages – in the case of children and in the case of old people.

PETS AND CHILDREN

Children get very attached to pets and watching a young child and a puppy or a kitten growing up together and helping each other is one of the great pleasures of family life.

However, there is much more to it than that. Pets help children to learn the important skill of communication without words and they also instill in them a respect for nature that can be very valuable. They serve as a very useful introduction to the experiences of life and death, and the sciences of biology, natural history and reproduction. Indeed, there are plans to incorporate pet animal studies into the school curriculum in the early 1990s as part of a GCSE science subject. Children are also able to learn about the responsibilities of ownership including feeding, grooming, exercising and care in ill health. Owning a pet can be a very useful social asset and help in developing self-confidence and friendships.

A recent study in Cambridge compared two groups of children, one of them pet owning and the other not. The main indications were quite clear: the pet owning families, the relationship between children and their parents was better and this led to a happier family atmosphere. In addition, the greater the number of pets owned, the better the child's social competence.

A study of cats in Switzerland took a different standpoint and looked at the human-cat relationship from the cat's point of view. It seemed that cats behaved differently towards different members of the family – boys, girls and adults. It also showed that the relationship between a child and a cat is markedly different from that between a child and a dog – so here again, it seems that there are very good psychological reasons for a child owning more than one pet.

Children can often find a common interest with older people through pets. The elderly can teach the

boarders. The best boarding kennels provide a good basic diet and are prepared for the occasional dog with a finicky appetite. If your dog has to have a special diet, discuss it with the kennel proprietor and, if necessary, arrange to bring a supply of food to the kennel. Most healthy dogs soon settle down in boarding kennels and enjoy the basic menu which they see all the others wolfing with apparent enjoyment. However, dogs with kidney problems, diabetic dogs, etc, may be better boarded with a veterinary surgeon.

The above recommendations may seem very complicated, but your dog is in no position to complain about anything he does not like. He is stuck with your choice of holiday for him, so the least you can do is to inspect his holiday hotel before making a reservation. Do not begrudge higher fees for superior care and bear in mind that the best kennels are usually booked well in advance. Once you have found a reliable boarding kennel, become a regular customer. Your dog will be more relaxed at a kennels he knows and will settle in more quickly.

> **A sure alliance**
>
> We are alone, absolutely alone on this chance planet, and, amid all the forms of life that surround us, not one, excepting the dog, has made an alliance with us.
>
> Maurice Maeterlinck

young a lot about pet care and where there is an age difference which can easily be 50 years, the love for the pet helps to bridge the 'generation gap'.

PETS AND THE ELDERLY

In recent years, as the quality of life has improved, so has the average life expectancy of people living in this country. Nowadays, older people are considerably more active than in previous generations and are finding that there is much to be enjoyed during the years of retirement.

Most old people still live in their own homes and a large proportion of them live alone. The most immediate advantage that pets offer to these people is companionship and this is all the more important when so much human contact is through the medium of technology, the phone, the radio and television, and with relatives often living hundreds of miles away. The actual extent of loneliness in a busy world can be enormous but this can be significantly reduced by owning a pet.

A dog can make the elderly feel safer alone at home and any pet can help in preventing the onset of mental confusion. At the simplest level, feeding the pet can remind the owner to feed him – or herself.

Another physical advantage that is often overlooked is that elderly people may keep their homes warmer for the sake of their pet than they would do if they lived alone, so keeping themselves warm. Even the smallest dog requires some exercise which should ensure that an older person goes out at least once a day, helping them to keep active. A pet can open up a whole new world for an older person and can give them a new appetite for life.

Obviously, the elderly should only undertake keeping the sort of pet that they can reasonably expect to look after. For most of them, a large dog would be out of the question but with even the smallest animal, the element of exercise can be vital to the owner. Even feeding a caged bird helps to exercise the shoulder muscles and stroking a cat can be beneficial to the chair-bound.

A pet can help to alleviate the problems of disability and infirmity by taking the person's mind off the affliction and it can also provide a distraction from depression or bereavement.

The very real advantages of pet ownership to the elderly are more widely recognised today and there are more and more schemes around the world for putting pets together with the elderly to improve the quality of their lives. A recent study in this country examined the effect of giving pet budgies to elderly people living on their own. What the study showed was that the pleasure that the birds gave to the owners amounted almost to a new lease of life. The participants quickly formed a very strong attachment to their pets and the presence of the birds made the owner more popular with young visitors. The study proved conclusively the value of these pets for the elderly in a very noticeable way – the birds proved to be far more rewarding companions than the one-way dialogue with the television. In short, pets have an enormous role to play in the later life of most people ... and the improvement in the quality of life that pets offer can be seen in the physical health and stability of the owner as much as in their emotional satisfaction.

Complementary Medicine for Dogs

The veterinarian practising holistic veterinary medicine aims to consider the spiritual, mental, emotional, and physical aspects of the life of his patients. The owner, or 'steward', who is responsible for the day to day care,will play a part in the same process.

All aspects of the dog's life are looked at, from feeding, exercise and play to previous illnesses, relationships with other human and animal members of the household. The 'holistic' veterinarian will need a greater degree of observation from the steward and more involvement with treatment.

Apart from orthodox medicine and surgery, there are a number of other forms of treatment and diagnosis, only some of which will be considered here. These vary from the ancient therapies of massage, nutrition, herbal medicine and acupuncture to the more recent developments of homoeopathy, radionics and iridology.

Sometimes these are known as alternative medicine, but the term complementary medicine is preferable, as this implies the use of the less orthodox methods in conjunction with modern medicine. The ideal would seem to operate when the veterinarian is able to consider the individual patient, and give advice based on knowledge of a whole range of therapies, including modern medicine. There is often a choice of courses of action and the holistic approach includes the client, the steward of the dog, in the process of making a decision. Indeed it is customary for the veterinarian to discuss the various options and then to leave the client to decide on what to do.

A principle that runs through all the traditions of complementary medicine is that the natural state is one of good health. In this state all parts of the being exist in harmony and balance. The very word 'health' is derived from a root word meaning whole.

One result of this outlook is greater attention to the way of life and diet, so that health is promoted and illness is less likely to occur.

MASSAGE

Massage starts naturally soon after birth when the bitch licks each pup. Licking the nostrils removes fluids and clears the airway for breath, but more importantly it stimulates nerve receptors which help to start and deepen the breathing of the new-born pup. Licking the

Opposite:
Smile please!

186

body dries the coat and reduces chilling, at the same time stimulating the sense of touch in the pup and increasing the return of blood from the veins. For the first few weeks, the dam licks the pups to induce the passing of urine and faeces which she swallows. Without this attention from the bitch the very young pups are not able to pass urine or faeces. This whole procedure ensures that the pups and the nest are kept clean.

As the pups grow older, the bitch will still lick and groom them from time to time, and this helps to build strong bonds of kinship and affection.

In the same way, stroking your dog conveys your affection, builds strong bonds between you, and helps to keep him relaxed and happy. Relaxation and happiness are closely related to good health.

More recently scientific studies have confirmed that these benefits work both ways, to improve human health and well-being. In studies on people prone to heart disease, stroking a dog can reduce the human heart rate.

Massage, particularly of the backbone and the adjacent muscles, has a beneficial effect that can be used as part of a health maintaining regimen for any dog. This can be extended down the legs and the feet to include the pads and between the toes, though some dogs may be ticklish here or elsewhere. The degree of strength to be used for massage will vary with the individual dog. A Chihuahua will need less than a Boxer, a pup less than an adult, the middle-aged less than the elderly. For ill or weakened dogs, massage should be gentle and not prolonged.

NUTRITION

Food and drink form the very substance from which the cells of the body are made, and thus determine the constitution of the fluids in which every cell in the body is bathed So sound nutrition is needed throughout life to maintain health.

Muscle meat such as beef, lamb, various fishes, chicken and rabbit can be fed. This can be balanced with about a sixth the amount of offal, among which liver is a good source of vitamin A (too much liver can cause toxicity.) There is less risk of contracting infection from meat if it is given cooked, though raw meat is more natural and healthy. Many people feed raw beef and lamb with no ill effects; factory farmed chicken should always be thoroughly cooked, but free-range birds fed a healthy diet are safe.

Vegetable roughage can be provided by the addition of certain finely grated raw, or cooked mashed vegetables (see page 93). Some cooked cereals can be fed. Special bone flour for dogs is a good source of calcium. Bones themselves need to be carefully selected for safety (see page 92).

Skill, knowledge and experience is needed to formulate a diet. Without expert guidance, it is best to feed proprietary tins and biscuit meal. Those from reputable manufacturers are formulated to supply a nutritionally balanced diet.

HERBALISM

Domestic dogs and their wild relations seek and eat plant material to maintain health and heal disease. The use of herbal medicine by mankind is one of the oldest forms of medicine which has probably been used as long as there have been illnesses. The use of herbs to treat domesticated animals has followed whenever these animals have been valued by man.

Different parts of the plants may be selected according to their various properties. Thus leaf, bud, bark, twig, fruit, seed, sap, resin, root, rhizome and root bark are variously used. Ancient wisdom knows the differing properties of the plants and modern research is increasingly confirming the traditional usage.

Fresh or dried plant material may be added to the food; tisanes and decoctions may be prepared and dosed by mouth or used locally on the skin or wounds; dried material and dried extracts are available in tablet form. For about a hundred years, medical herbalists treating human patients have made much use of extracts in alcoholic solutions; extracts in water and glycerin have been widely used by the author and found to be effective, as well as being acceptable to the majority of canine patients.

This German Spitz looks game for anything

> **A prayer**
>
> 'God give to me by your grace what you give to dogs by nature.'
>
> Mechtilda of Magdeberg, a thirteenth-century hermitess

Anyone for a snowball fight?

Herbs can be used to treat a wide variety of conditions. It is well known that *Salix alba*, the bark of white willow, contains salicylates, the substances that inspired the manufacture of aspirin. However, there are salicylates in other willows and many other herbal remedies, all of which provide a safe way of relieving pain.

Many herbs have different functions which are quite varied. For example motherwort, used in the treatment of heart disease, is also used to increase fertility in the female, and to increase the contraction of the uterus during whelping. It follows that this herbal remedy should not be given during pregnancy.

A skin wound might need some *Achillea millefolium* (yarrow) to control minor haemorrhage; then, later, some *Thymus vulgaris* (thyme) to help control infection and encourage the growth of fibrous tissue; later still, the addition of some *Symphytum officinale* (comfrey) to promote the final stage of healing.

These few examples are a brief introduction to a vast and fascinating subject. The remedies are all safe if used correctly and the dose needed is many times smaller than that which would cause harmful effects. The dose varies from a few milligrams for the more toxic plants to a few grams for the more commonly used safer remedies; variation is made for breed, age and the strength of the patient and also for nature of the condition being treated and the stage of the illness.

HOMOEOPATHY

It is an old-established principle that a substance which in relatively large doses causes certain symptoms, can be used in much smaller doses to treat similar symptoms in a patient. The modern practice of homoeopathy is a particular development and refinement of this principle, made in the late eighteenth century, by Dr Samuel Hahnemann. In its simplest form the selection of the remedy is guided by the phrase 'let like be cured by like'.

The remedy is used in an extremely diluted form. Homoeopaths believe that the potency of the remedy is increased at each stage of dilution by means of a vigorous shaking procedure called succussion. Starting with an alcoholic solution, the mother tincture with a concentration of about one part in three is diluted in stages either by tenfold or one hundredfold dilutions.

The potency 6 is most readily available. This is a dilution of one part in 1,000,000,000,000 of the mother tincture. It follows that the amount of the original material is extremely small. At a potency of 12 there are theoretically no molecules of the original material, only the energy remains.

The remedies used vary from herbs to inorganic substances such as chemical compounds; from substances of animal origin such as snake venom to pharmaceutical compounds which may have been previously used with ill effects, eg, corticosteroids. The considerable dilutions mean that there is no risk of any harm to patients.

At first sight the whole concept of homoeopathic medicine may appear unconvincing and would seem to provide a fertile field for chicanery. Against this must be weighed the practical evidence of the many patients who are helped, often when orthodox measures have failed. Most of the veterinarians who use this form of diagnosis and therapy are remarkable for their probity and general level of competence.

ACUPUNCTURE

The system of acupuncture currently practised in the West had its origins about seven hundred years ago in China. Adaptation for veterinary application is recent but the principles are the same.

Newsworthy

When a dog bites a man that is not new, but when a man bites a dog that is new.

Charles A. Dana

A test of conscience

If a dog will not come to you after he has looked you in the face, you ought to go home and examine your conscience.

Woodrow Wilson

Flea distraction

They say a reasonable amount o' fleas is good fer a dog – keeps him from broodin' over bein' a dog mebbee.

Edward N. Westcott

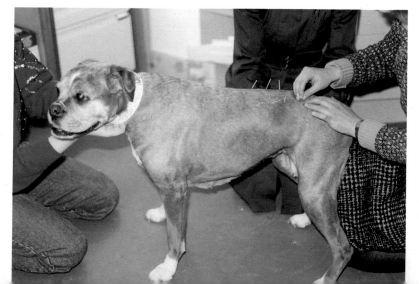

Elderly Boxer being treated by acupuncture for arthritis

Fine needles are used to puncture the skin. This is done at varying points on the body according to the needs of the patient. The points lie along lines called meridians. Traditionally it is said that the treatment adjusts the energies in the body, returning them to the state of balance that is health. Other methods of stimulation such as ultrasonic energy, electrical current and even laser light beams are now used with varying degrees of success. These less traumatic methods have obvious advantages for restless or uncooperative patients, though it must be said that it is surprising how well the treatment with needles is tolerated by many patients.

It is interesting that the acupuncture points on the ancient charts can be shown to coincide with places on the skin that have decreased electrical resistance when investigated by modern technology. A correlation has also been demonstrated with various underlying structures of the peripheral nervous system.

In veterinary medicine acupuncture has been found useful in a variety of conditions. It is most used for conditions of the vertebral column and also for some dysfunctions of the nervous system.

PHYSIOTHERAPY

Injury to bones, muscles, joints and tendons causes pain and impairs movement. General health and various internal organs may also be affected.

These injuries may be treated by a variety of complementary therapies but the addition of selected techniques of physiotherapy can be a great help. Rest and graded exercise according to the needs of the patient are the priority. Massage has been mentioned above. Application of cold or heat can be useful.

As with all methods of treatment, knowledge and experience are essential. This becomes more obvious when machines that are now available are used. Misuse is potentially very damaging. Used correctly, techniques such as short-wave diathermy, ultrasound and electrical stimulation of muscle groups, can make a real contribution.

Some physiotherapists who are fully trained and qualified for human treatment also work in conjunction with veterinarians. Most experience has been gained with the treatment of horses but some with racing greyhounds. As with human patients, there is no reason why this therapy should be limited to athletes.

Opposite:

Playing it cool – the wanted look

If you are looking for a new master, it doesn't do to make a fuss. A touch of softness won't hurt, and makes those faces at the wire take another look: better to play it cool and let your good looks do the work. And it did work for Angel – hardly surprising, really – she *is* big, but her heart's big, too.

Freddie Reed

DOG SIZES GUIDE

SPORTING (Hounds, Gundogs, Terriers)

Hounds

Hounds	Height at shoulder (inches)	Weight (lbs)
Afghan	25 – 29	
Basenji	16 – 17	22 – 24
Basset	13 – 15	
Beagle	13 – 16	
Bloodhound	23 – 27	
Borzoi	27 +	
Dachshund (Smooth-haired)		23 – 25
(Long-haired)		17 – 18
(Wire-haired)		18 – 22
Dachshund – Miniature (Smooth, Wire, Long,)		10
Deerhound	28 – 30	65
Elkhound	19 – 20	43 – 50
Finnish Spitz	15 – 17	
Greyhound	27 – 30	
Ibizan	22 – 28	
Irish Wolfhound	28 +	90 +
Otterhound	23 – 27	
Petit Basset Griffon Vendeen	13 – 15	
Pharaoh	21 – 25	
Rhodesian Ridgeback	24 – 27	70 – 80
Saluki	23 – 28	
Whippet	17 – 18	20

Foxhounds (English) – never seen at KC shows, but are kept in packs and have their own shows organised by Masters of Foxhounds

23

Harriers – also never shown   18 – 22

Gundogs

Gundogs	Height	Weight
English Setter	24 – 27	55 – 70
Gordon Setter	24 – 26	55 – 65
Irish Setter	25 – 27	60 – 70
Irish Red & White Setter	24 – 27	55 – 70
German Short-haired Pointer	21 – 25	45 – 70
German Wire-haired Pointer	24 – 26	
Hungarian Vizsla	21 – 25	48 – 66
Large Munsterlander	24	60
Pointer	24 – 27	
Retriever (Curlycoat)	25 – 27	70 – 80
Retriever (Flatcoat)		60 – 70
Retriever (Golden)	20 – 24	55 – 70
Retriever (Labrador)	21 – 22	
Spaniel (American Cocker)	14 – 15	22 – 28
Spaniel (Clumber)		45 – 70
Spaniel (Cocker)	15 – 16	28 – 32
Spaniel (English Springer)	20	50
Spaniel (Field)	18	35 – 50
Spaniel (Irish Water)	21 – 24	
Spaniel (Sussex)	15 – 16	40 – 50
Spaniel (Welsh Springer)	18 – 19	35 – 45
Weimeraner	22 – 27	

Terriers

Terriers	Height	Weight
Airedale	22 – 24	
Australian	10	10 – 11
Bedlington	16	
Border		11 – 15
Bull		
Bull (Miniature)	14	20
Cairn	9 – 10	13 – 14
Dandie Dinmont	8 – 11	18 – 24
Fox Terrier (Smooth)		15 – 18
Fox Terrier (Wire)	15	18
Irish	18	25 – 27
Kerry Blue	18 – 19	33 – 37
Lakeland	14	15 – 17
Manchester	15 – 16	
Norfolk	10	
Norwich	10	10
Scottish	10 – 11	19 – 23
Sealyham	8 – 12	18 – 20
Skye	10	25
Soft Coated Wheaten	18 – 19	35 – 45
Staffordshire Bull	14 – 16	24 – 38
Welsh	15	20
West Highland White	11	
Jack Russell Terriers	13 – 14	

NON-SPORTING (Utility, Working, Toy)

Utility

Utility	Height	Weight
Boston Terrier		25
Bulldog		50 – 55
Chow Chow	18	
Dalmatian	22 – 24	
French Bulldog		24 – 28
Japanese Spitz	10 – 16	13
Keeshond	17 – 18	
Lhasa Apso	10	
Poodle (Miniature)	11 – 15	
(Standard)	15 +	
(Toy)	under 11	
Schipperke	12 – 13	12 – 16
Schnauzer (Standard)	18 – 19	
(Miniature)	13 – 14	
Shih Tzu	10	10 – 18
Tibetan Spaniel	10	9 – 15
Tibetan Terrier	14 – 16	

List of Breeds in their Groups, as recognised by the Kennel Club

Working

Bearded Collie	20 – 22	
Bernese Mountain Dog	24 – 27	
Border Collie	17 – 18	
Bouvier des Flandres	23 – 27	
Boxer	21 – 24	
Briard	22 – 27	
Bullmastiff	24 – 27	90 – 130
Collie (Rough)	20 – 24	
(Smooth)	20 – 24	
Dobermann	25 – 27	
German Shepherd Dog		
(Alsatian)	22 – 26	
Giant Schnauzer	23 – 27	
Great Dane	28 +	100 +
Belgian Shepherd Dog		
(Groenendael)	22 – 26	
Hungarian Puli	14 – 18	
Maremma Sheepdog	23 – 26	
Mastiff	27 +	
Newfoundland	26 – 28	
Norwegian Buhund	under 18	
Old English Sheepdog	22	
Pyrenean	26 – 28	
Rottweiler	23 – 27	
St Bernard	25 +	
(the bigger the better)		
Samoyed	18 – 22	
Shetland Sheepdog	14	
Siberian Husky	20 – 23	40 – 60
Swedish Vallhund	12 – 13	
Belgian Shepherd Dog		
(Tervueren)	24	
Welsh Corgi (Cardigan)	12	20 – 26
(Pembroke)	10 – 12	18 – 24

Toy

Bichon Frisé	9 – 11	
Cavalier King Charles Spaniel		10 – 18
Chihuahua (Longcoat)		2 – 6
(Smoothcoat)		2 – 6
Chinese Crested		7 – 12
English Toy Terrier		
(Black & Tan)	10 – 12	6 – 8
Griffon Bruxellois		5 – 11
Italian Greyhound		6 – 8
Japanese Chin	'dainty'	7
King Charles Spaniel		6 – 12
Löwchen (Little Lion Dog)		8 – 9
Maltese	10	
Miniature Pinscher	10 12	
Papillon	8 – 11	
Pekingese		7 – 12

Pomeranian		4 – 5
Pug		14 – 18
Yorkshire Terrier		7

Some Rare Breeds

Alaskan Malamute	23 – 25	85 – 125
Anatolian Shepherd Dog	30	100 – 110
Australian Cattle Dog	18 – 20	
Australian Silky Terrier	9	8 – 10
Affenpinscher	9 – 11	7 – 8
Belgian Shepherd Dog		
(Laekenois)	22 – 26	
(Malinois)	22 – 26	
Canaan Dog	24	60
Eskimo Dog	20 – 25	50 – 90
Estrela Mountain Dog	24 – 28	
German Spitz (Klein)	9 – 11	
(Mittel)	11 14	
Glen of Imaal	14	30 – 35
Grand Bleu de Gascogne		
Hamilton Stovare	18 – 23	
Hovawart	23 – 27	
Italian Spinone	23 – 27	70 – 80
Japanese Akita	23 – 27	
Komondor	23 – 31	80 – 135
Kooikerhondje	14 – 16	
Leonburger	27 – 30	100
Lancashire Heeler	12	
Pinscher	12	
Portuguese Water Dog	21	46
Retriever (Chesapeake Bay)	20 – 26	55 – 75
(Nova Scotia Duck Tolling)	18 – 20	35 – 55
Shar-Pei		
Shiba Inu	15 – 17	25 – 35
Spaniel (Brittany)	17 – 20	30 – 40
Tibetan Mastiff	27 – 28	130

**All sizes (where given) are approximate but will enable you to judge if the dog will knock things off the coffee table with its tail, be able to commandeer your best chair, or take up more of your bed than you do!

A-Z of Dog's Health

Abortion Sound diet and steady exercise help to prevent abortion in healthy bitches. Violence, brucellosis, herpes virus and toxoplasmosis infections are likely to cause abortion.

Abrasion Leave uncovered after thorough cleansing with warm saline solution. Regularly examine the wound for signs of increasing inflammation or tenderness and keep it dry while new skin layers form.

Abscess Apply fairly hot salt-water fomentations to relieve pain. The infection itself may require antibiotic treatment from a veterinarian.

Adhesion Abnormal sticking together of organs or membranes, sometimes following an inflammatory condition in abdominal cavity, lungs, joints etc. Surgery may be required to correct.

Albuminuria Albumin present in the urine indicates early kidney inflammation and cystitis. The urine is very cloudy and a laboratory test will confirm.

Allergy Common allergens include fleas and other parasites. Some dogs may be allergic to cow's milk, eggs, pork, fish etc, or to pollens, insect stings, specific antibiotics or some hormone treatments. Allergies can also stem from contact with certain types of bedding or carpet materials, rubber products, household sprays and airborne cleaning fluids. Symptoms include sneezing, weeping of eyes, skin rash, or swelling.

Administer antihistamines while tracking down the cause. Preparations containing various mixtures of calamine, coal tar and sulphur can be beneficial. An 'Elizabethan Collar' will help stop a patient from chewing or licking an exposed area.

Alopecia Loss of hair due to a nutritional deficiency, selenium poisoning or, more frequently, hormone imbalance. In males it sometimes indicates a tumour of the testicle. Hormone treatment is usually prescribed.

Anaemia Symptoms include weakness, pale visible mucous membranes (eyelids, gums etc), a pounding heart, dull coat, reduced appetite and, subsequently, emaciation. A balanced, nutritious diet helps to prevent anaemia. If vitamins are used, careful veterinary control of intake is needed. A possible cause of anaemia can be parasites.

Anal glands These two glands (situated just below and to each side of the anus) sometimes become obstructed and consequently inflamed. The dog may chase its tail, yelp when sitting down and drag its tail end along the ground. Relief can be obtained by gently but firmly pressing a pad of lint or cotton wool against the anus and, by pressure of finger and thumb on either side of the anus, squeezing the obstructing matter out. The technique is best demonstrated by a veterinarian. There may be an abscess present which will need antibiotic treatment.

Arthritis The pain of arthritis varies from a dull ache to evident discomfort and restricted movement. It occurs sometimes in aged dogs. Make sure the dog is comfortable, well dried after a wet walk, has draught-free sleeping quarters and is considered with patience when the joints are stiff. Aspirin is sometimes prescribed and cortisone may be given in extreme cases. Arthritis often attacks heavier, fatter dogs with some severity – the additional weight adds to pain and discomfort.

Ascaridae A class of internal parasites commonly known as roundworms (*see* parasites).

Ascites Fluid gathering in the abdomen. Swelling is usually evident. It is a symptom of various diseases, including heart, kidney and liver diseases, tumours, tuberculosis and diabetes. It can also arise from the presence of an internal parasitic infestation. Early diagnosis by a veterinarian is of great importance.

Aspergillosis A fungal disease which dogs can contract from poultry. The spores of the fungus can be present in hay, grain, etc, and are inhaled. They multiply and thrive in the tissues, chiefly in the nasal passages, producing a cheesy discharge which clogs the breathing organs. The fungus reproduces and the condition worsens. Muzzle rubbing, a nasal discharge (often bloody) and distress are symptoms. Sometimes convulsions occur. The condition needs veterinary attention. Fresh air and a sound diet will assist in recovery.

Asthma Symptoms of asthma and chronic bronchitis are similar, though asthma usually occurs irregularly and is accompanied by sudden attacks of difficult, spasmodic breathing lasting for several minutes. Distress is evident. Stress and allergies are possible causes. Some breeds appear to be more susceptible than others.

Asthma is difficult to treat with drugs since it is rarely possible to get a dog to inhale to order. Eliminate any stress, investigate a possible allergy and maintain a sound diet with regular exercise.

Ataxia Defective muscle control or co-ordination, which can be hereditary, appearing sometimes in Jack Russell or Fox Terriers around four months old. It can be symptomatic of various nervous disorders, including encephalitis, meningitis and brain tumours. Consult a veterinarian.

Backache Any back pain requires a veterinary examination since there may be a variety of causes – some of a serious nature. It may be muscular, or due to a spinal or skeletal disorder (eg, hip dysplasia), or it could be the symptom of an internal problem such as kidney disease. Some gynaecological conditions are reflected in back pain. If muscular or skeletal in origin it will almost certainly be worsened by obesity.

Belching While a dog belching at the end of a meal indicates a sufficiency, constant belching at other times may indicate a stomach disorder such as indigestion.

Bites The seriousness of a bite cannot be measured in relation to the size since a small deep puncture may produce an infection or internal damage. A dog bitten in a fight should always be examined by a veterinarian.

Blepharitis Inflammation of the eyelids which may or may not be caused by conjunctivitis. Bathe eyes gently with warm water and if there is no improvement within a day or two consult a veterinarian who will probably prescribe eye drops or ointments.

Blindness Canine blindness can be hereditary or caused by disease or injury. A blind dog can still be happy with extra care: keep furniture in exactly the same place and train the dog to respond immediately on command. 'Crash helmets' have been made from leather muzzles to give added protection.

Bronchitis There are acute and chronic forms of this disease. Infections and worsening colds or chills are the usual origins of the acute form.

Chronic bronchitis is often the result of an untreated acute attack, especially in aged and overweight dogs. Keep the affected dog warm, quiet, away from cold and draughts, and feed a diet of easily digestible, palatable food. See a veterinarian as soon as possible.

Bronchopneumonia While bronchitis attacks the larger air passages, pneumonia affects the minute breathing vessels inside, clogging them with fluid. It can be the result of worsening bronchitis, or a secondary infection. Respiratory distress is evident and sometimes a cough and nasal discharge appear. Keep the dog warm and still and obtain veterinary treatment quickly. A nutritious, easily digested diet and compassionate nursing will speed recovery.

Calculus A stone which forms from the accumulation of mineral salts in body fluids. It is most commonly found in the urinary system (kidneys, bladder etc), the gall bladder and bile duct. Symptoms are pain or marked tenderness in the appropriate region. There is often an obstruction which may necessitate surgical removal.

Cancer There are various forms of cancer which affect the dog. The most common occurs in the mammary glands of the bitch. Regular examination will help to detect growths in their early stages and maximise recovery chances. Surgical removal is often recommended.

Canker A general term for ear disease, more common in flap-eared dogs. The dog shakes its head and hangs it to one side. A brown, sticky wax can usually be seen, accompanied by inflammation. Sometimes there is a smelly discharge. Canker is frequently caused by ear mites and occurs in both dry and wet forms.

Veterinary treatment is necessary – ear drops are usually prescribed. (Do not use proprietary powders which clog the ear and cannot drain out.) Clean the outside of the ear gently with cotton wool, but do not poke around inside the ear. Warm the drops slightly (to body temperature), and drop them in with the head held on one side. Close the ear and gently massage.

Prevention of chronic canker means regular inspection to arrest the condition in its early stages. Keep the outer ear dry and clear of matted hair at all times.

Car sickness Some dogs are distressed by the motion of a moving vehicle. They will salivate, pant and whine restlessly. Familiarise the dog with the car over short journeys and/or sit in the motionless car and soothe the dog gently. This condition usually improves with patience and understanding as the dog grows up.

Cataract The lens of the eye becomes opaque and a film can be seen over the eye. Dimness of vision is followed by loss of sight though this may take some considerable time. This condition is most common in elderly dogs and, while surgery is often recommended in younger animals, this may not be advisable in an old dog, especially if some sight remains.

Catarrh Nasal catarrh usually occurs as a result of cold, damp conditions and can deteriorate to produce more serious respiratory problems, symptomised by a nasal discharge and sometimes a fever. Veterinary assistance will be needed to fight such an infection.

Chill Chills, shown by prolonged feverish shivering, often arise from the dog remaining wet in cold conditions. They can worsen to produce bronchitis and other serious conditions. Always ensure your dog is well dried after being exposed to cold, wet conditions and keep it warm and dry for a while afterwards to stabilise its body temperature.

Choking Prevention is vital, as choking often proves fatal due to the difficulty of removing an obstruction from the throat of a panicking dog. Ensure that the dog is not fed unsuitable bones and does not have access to small toys or other objects. Puppies are especially vulnerable.

If choking occurs, grasp the dog's tongue, pull it forward and attempt to remove the foreign body with your fingers.

Colitis Inflammation of the colon or large intestine, usually caused by a foreign body or infection. Pain and tenderness in the abdominal region will be evident. Veterinary attention is necessary.

Conjunctivitis Inflammation of the eye causing watering and often a gummy discharge. It is caused by an infection, dust/grit in the eye, smoke or pollen. Wash gently with a warm saline solution and seek veterinary treatment if it does not clear up in a day or two. Antibiotics may be needed to fight the infection.

Constipation This is frequently due to an incorrect diet but can be symptomatic of something more serious. A 50/50 mixture of castor and olive oils, or a little syrup of figs can be given as a mild laxative.

Coughing Regular coughing fits may indicate an infection or even a heart disorder (*see also* kennel cough).

Cystitis Symptoms are frequent passing of urine and associated pain. Consult a veterinarian, taking a fresh urine sample in a clean container.

Deafness It is not uncommon for aged dogs to become deaf. When they do, more patience and understanding are essential. A deaf dog will not hear traffic coming, and a previously obedient dog will gradually cease to respond to commands. Most dogs will learn to recognise hand signals but their attention must be gained by a light tap on the body. Care of a dog's ears throughout its life helps to prevent deafness.

Dehydration This very serious condition is the frequent result of untreated diarrhoea, vomiting, heat exhaustion, etc, where fluid loss is greater than intake. Over-exercising a dog in hot weather can also cause dehydration which, if not corrected quickly, can cause death. Give a glucose saline solution (1 level tsp salt plus 1 heaped tbsp glucose powder in ½pt boiled, cooled water) and consult a veterinarian.

Diabetes An overweight dog which rapidly loses weight and becomes thirsty, with fits of trembling and restlessness, should be considered a possible diabetic. Consult a veterinarian.

Diarrhoea Frequent diarrhoea is dangerous as it can lead to dehydration. Temporary diarrhoea less than two days is probably due to diet, eg, too much liver or a sudden change. Some dogs cannot tolerate certain foods. Withhold solid food for 24-48 hours, giving only glucose water (2tbsp glucose in ¼pt boiled and cooled water). Try beating in a raw egg towards the end of the period. Feed bland foods such as boiled rice and chicken breasts for a few days afterwards to allow the digestive system time to settle.

Distemper A serious, highly infectious viral disease which attacks the nervous system and frequently proves fatal. Prevention is by immunisation in puppyhood. No dog should be allowed in public before it has been immunised.

Ectropion Turning outwards of the eyelid, possibly hereditary, causing discomfort to an affected dog. Minor surgery can correct.

Eczema This skin inflammation is often due to an allergy. There are wet and dry forms, both of which cause substantial irritation, with the patient biting and scratching affected areas.

While trying to trace the cause of the condition, relieve the irritation and avoid skin damage by carefully removing surrounding hair, cleansing the area with a warm saline solution and applying a suitable lotion, eg, a mixture of coal tar, calamine and sulphur. A veterinarian may prescribe antihistamine injections and can often help trace the cause.

Entropion Turning in of the eyelid, causing discomfort. Corrective surgery is needed as soon as possible.

Epilepsy Often hereditary. A mild form can occur in some puppies while cutting teeth or during an infestation of intestinal parasites. It can be triggered by hysteria or stress and produces convulsions, incontinence and sometimes complete loss of consciousness. Afterwards the patient may be confused and will need quiet and low light. If recurring, consult a veterinarian.

Exposure Underfed dogs subjected to severe weather conditions are especially liable to suffer from exposure. A teaspoonful of cod liver oil mixed into food will help outdoor dogs during winter.

Fever A serious health problem is signalled by a body temperature of over 41.7°C (107°F). An increase to 42.8°C (109°F) is life threatening if the fever is prolonged. Symptoms include distress or lethargy, loss of appetite, increased breathing rate etc. Consult a veterinarian without delay.

Fracture Veterinary attention is needed urgently. Prolonged pain may worsen to a shock condition and handling must be extremely gentle. A temporary splint can be applied with padding between limb and splint. Keep the patient still, warm and comfortable until the veterinarian arrives. Careful nursing is important after the fracture has been set.

Gastroenteritis There are many causes of gastroenteritis, symptomised by pain, excessive diarrhoea and possibly vomiting. Veterinary treatment is essential, followed by gentle and attentive nursing until the patient has fully recovered. Offer bland foods such as chicken breasts and boiled rice until the dog's strength has fully returned.

Glaucoma An eye condition characterised by impaired sight and swelling of the eyeball. Surgery is often needed.

Grass seed invasion For flap-eared dogs particularly, some grass seeds can be very dangerous. During the summer months such grasses as barley and brome can become implanted in ears as well as between a dog's toes and inside nostrils. Their presence causes great pain and often infection. Attempts should not be made to extract the seeds from deep inside ears or nostrils without the expertise of a veterinarian.

Haematoma A swelling filled with blood which is caused by rupture of a blood vessel. A common cause of this in flap-eared dogs is continual head shaking and scratching due to irritation inside the ear (*see also* canker) or the presence of parasites there. Haematomas can also be produced from a violent blow and will probably require surgical draining.

Heat stroke An extremely dangerous, possibly fatal, condition. One of the most common causes is shutting a dog in a car exposed to direct sunlight. The interior of the car will heat up to unbearable temperatures within minutes and a dog confined inside will have little chance of survival. Cars should always be left in shade with windows open sufficiently to admit air ('grills' can be purchased to fit in the space). A bowl of water should always be left in the car.

Dogs left out in sunlight without access to shade and cool water are also vulnerable to heat stroke.

Symptoms are: panting, distress, increased breathing rate, vomiting, diarrhoea and convulsions. Internal bleeding may occur before the dog finally dies. Take the dog into the shade and bathe gently in cold water to reduce the body temperature. Call a veterinarian immediately, as there will almost certainly be complications, including dehydration.

Hepatitis This viral disease is prevented by immunisation during puppyhood. Hepatitis is usually lethal. Symptoms include bloody diarrhoea, vomiting, listlessness, abdominal pain and fever.

Herpes Viral disease associated with the genitalia of the bitch, but it can infect puppies or adult dogs. Symptoms include sores on the nose and vaginal inflammation. Prescribed ointments will help. Avoid secondary site infection.

Hip dysplasia Largely hereditary disease affecting some strains of some breeds. The hip joint becomes dislocated and deformed. Pain will be noticed during exercise and when rising from a sitting position. Surgery may be necessary.

Hookworm An intestinal parasite which sucks the blood (*see also* parasites).

Infection An infection should be treated by a veterinarian as soon as possible. Symptoms include fever, high temperature, general lethargy, dull eyes and coat.

Interdigital cysts These cysts occur quite commonly between the dog's toes. They are frequently pus-filled and will usually be noticed through the dog continually licking between the toes. Some tenderness of the foot will also be apparent. Keep the foot clean to prevent a secondary infection. If cysts do not heal quickly, or recur, consult a veterinarian.

Jaundice Symptoms of jaundice include a yellowish tinge in eyes, gums and inside of the mouth, clay-coloured faeces, lethargy and possibly vomiting. The dog becomes slowly but progressively weaker and may become constipated. Jaundice may be indicative of hepatitis, liver or gall bladder damage, blood disease or poisoning. Consult a veterinarian urgently.

Kennel cough Viral respiratory infection which often disappears after about ten days, if the dog is in good general health. As it is an airborne virus it will spread quickly in confined spaces, such as kennels – hence its common name. Consult your veterinarian about immunisation.

Leptospirosis A serious disease usually spread in the

urine of infected rats, although transmission from one dog to another is common, particularly in kennels. It is generally fatal, so immunisation in puppyhood is essential. Infected dogs have jaundice with foul smelling faeces and probably some intestinal bleeding.

Mange Highly contagious skin infection caused by parasites. There are two forms, both equally serious with the possibility of secondary infection. Consult a veterinarian urgently.

During treatment all bedding should be burnt and replaced with clean newspaper which can be changed frequently and similarly disposed of.

Metritis Inflammation of the uterus after giving birth. Often, though not always, there is a foul-smelling discharge from the vagina with a fever and some vomiting. The bitch will be lethargic and depressed. A hysterectomy may be necessary and the pups will need to be hand-reared. A veterinary check to clear the uterus after whelping is an important preventive measure.

Nephritis This inflammatory condition of the kidneys is symptomised by increased thirst, loss of appetite, raised temperature, difficulty in walking, vomiting and, later, loss of weight. Aged dogs, particularly those exposed to damp, chill conditions, are prone, as are bitches with an untreated vaginal infection.

During veterinary treatment the patient should be carefully nursed in a warm, draught-free place with a special diet of chicken breasts, boneless fish, etc, in small amounts several times a day. Give clean, cool water in small quantities. Milk, honey and glucose are beneficial.

Obesity A fat dog is much more likely to have health problems. Excess weight puts strain on the back, heart, kidneys, lungs and other internal organs, lessening the resistance to infection and reducing lifespan. Keep your dog slim with a balanced diet and plenty of exercise. Elderly dogs are susceptible to obesity, so take care weight is not gained as the dog gets older. Consult your veterinarian before starting a reducing diet.

Pain A dog in pain may be lethargic or restless, with a glazed, unhappy look in its eyes. A dog in severe pain will be extremely distressed, whimpering or yelping, especially when the affected area is touched or disturbed. It may be panting as its rate of breathing increases. Note all symptoms and contact a veterinarian quickly.

Paralysis Paralysis can be partial, total, temporary or permanent – the outlook is not always as grim as it may at first appear. Causes include a back or head injury, distemper, a brain tumour or a chemical deficiency. If recovery is possible, soothing, encouraging nursing will be especially important. A paralysed dog will need to be turned several times a day to avoid body sores and lung congestion.

Parasites There are ectoparasites (external) and endoparasites (internal).

Ectoparasites include the familiar dog flea which does not spend its entire life cycle on the dog but inhabits bedding and other corners, causing irritation and sometimes eczema. It also carries an endoparasite in the form of tapeworm eggs which can get into the dog's intestine. Tapeworm eggs are also carried by some lice which have flat, brown or whitish bodies. Their strong claws hook into the skin where they remain for life, laying eggs on individual hairs and taking blood from the dog.

Both lice and fleas can be destroyed by an appropriate veterinary shampoo. Often a louse, or the equally aggressive tick, can be detached from its host by dripping a few drops of eucalyptus oil directly on it. Flea collars are of help to some dogs. Tell-tale droppings (like grains of coal dust in the dog's skin and fur) provide evidence of the presence of ectoparasites, together with the irritation they produce for the dog.

The most common endoparasite is the roundworm. An infestation can cause vomiting, internal pain, loss of weight, obstruction and even convulsions. Treatment and prevention is usually by worming tablets which can be mixed with food. Dogs who have access to rubbish or carrion, or who live with hunting cats are especially vulnerable. If worms appear in the faeces dose immediately, and regularly at 4-6 month intervals. Puppies should be wormed at about 3 or 4 weeks and again at 2 and 3 months.

A sound diet and regular grooming are helpful in protecting the dog against both types of parasite.

Parvo virus This highly dangerous disease has claimed many canine lives and is easily passed from one dog to another. Every dog should be immunised against it in puppyhood, and should receive regular booster injections.

Symptoms include severe diarrhoea, gastroenteritis, severe pain and associated bleeding. Dehydration rapidly follows and the stricken dog becomes progressively weaker.

Rabies A very infectious viral disease which produces a form of madness followed by death. It attacks the nervous system and can be contracted by a variety of warm-blooded creatures, including man. It is difficult to diagnose in the early stages and the incubation period varies with individuals. Fortunately, the disease has been prevented in the UK by quarantine regulations.

Rheumatism A general term covering painful disorders of muscles or joints for which there is no real cure, though analgesics will help to relieve pain. It is usually brought on by damp and cold conditions, affecting aged dogs particularly. Dry dogs thoroughly after a wet walk and ensure that living conditions are warm and draught-free to help prevent rheumatism.

Ringworm Fungal skin disease which causes irritation

and sometimes a yellowish crust on the affected areas. Hair generally falls out in circular patches. Consult a veterinarian.

Shock Shock affects many organs and life functions and can be fatal. Heavy haemorrhages or extensive burns are common causes. It must be dealt with quickly by a veterinarian.

Symptoms include rapid heart-beat, shallow breathing, weakness, shivering, vomiting, dilated pupils and confusion. Soothe the dog and keep it calm while awaiting a veterinarian.

Sprain A sudden, awkward movement of a joint can cause a sprain. Rest and cold compresses help to relieve the discomfort and analgesics may be needed if the pain is severe. A supporting bandage can be beneficial.

Stings Dogs, especially puppies, tend to investigate buzzing noises and then may be stung in the mouth. If a bee or wasp is swallowed and stings the throat, there is a danger of suffocation from the swelling.

Paws may also be stung, perhaps by jelly-fish and other sea creatures if the dog is romping on a seashore.

Bee stings should be removed if possible. The site of the sting should then be swabbed with a bicarbonate of soda solution. Keep an eye on the dog that has been stung, since some are more seriously affected.

.

Stroke Symptoms of stroke include some distress prior to the attack followed by a loss of balance and some paralysis. A continuous to-and-fro movement of the eyeballs is often observed. Keep the patient soothed and quiet in a darkened room and call a veterinarian.

Tartar This brownish deposit builds up on teeth that are unscaled, causing bad breath and, potentially, gum disease. If necessary, a veterinarian can scale and clean the dog's teeth under anaesthetic.

Thirst Excessive thirst can be a symptom of fever, diabetes, and other illnesses. It may even be due to stress.

Ulcer Ulcers vary considerably, from corneal ulcers in the eye to those on the surface of mammary tumours. They may also occur in the mouth, giving rise to bad breath and some pain on eating. A bed-ridden animal may develop ulcers on its body if not turned frequently. Neglected ulcers spread and suppurate, so consult a veterinarian at the first signs.

Vomiting Repeated vomiting is a dangerous symptom. Consult a veterinarian quickly. If vomiting does not recur the dog may merely have eaten something disagreeable, but monitor him carefully in case it is a symptom of something more serious.

Wounds All wounds should be taken seriously, for the damage they have already done and for the infection that can result from them. Deep wounds (however small) require urgent treatment by a veterinarian who will also check for internal damage.

Maximum cleanliness must be observed when handling or dressing wounds. Small, superficial wounds should be cleansed with a warm saline solution, after the hair surrounding the wound has been clipped away. (Cover the wound with a piece of clean gauze soaked in boiled, warm water to prevent any hairs falling into the wound as you clip.) Check the wound twice a day: it should remain pink and clean as it heals. Inflammation or suppuration indicate infection. If the paw is wounded a special bandage will be needed to keep the area clean.

USEFUL ADDRESSES

The Kennel Club
1 Clarges Street
Piccadilly, London W1Y 8AB
Tel: 071 629 5828

British Veterinary Association
7 Mansfield Street
London W1M OAT
Tel: 071 636 6541

National Canine Defence League
1 Pratt Mews
London NW1 OAD
Tel: 071 388 0137

PRO-Dogs National Charity/PAT Dogs
Rocky Bank
4 New Road
Ditton
Kent ME20 7AD
Tel: 0732 848499

Dog Breeders' Insurance Co Ltd
9 St Stephens Court
St Stephens Road
Bournemouth BH2 6LG
Tel: 0202 295771

The Animal Welfare Trust
Tyler's Way
Watford By-Pass
Watford
Herts WD2 8HQ
Tel: 081 950 8215

The Dogs Home Battersea
4 Battersea Park Road
London
SW8 4AA
Tel: 071 622 3626

Search and Rescue Dogs Association (SARDA)
Bridge House
Main Street
Keswick
Cumbria
Tel: 0596 72833

Guide Dogs for the Blind Association
Alexandra House
9 Park Street
Windsor, Berks SL4 1JR
Tel: 0753 855711

Hearing Dogs for the Deaf (Training Centre)
London Road
Lewknor
Oxon OX9 5RY
Tel: 0844 53898

Assistance Dogs for Disabled People
South: 23 Slipper Road
Emsworth
Hants PO10 8BS
Tel: 0243 375723
North: The Mount Veterinary Surgery
1 Harris Street
Fleetwood, Lancs FY7 6QX
Tel: 0391 75547

Dogs for the Disabled
Brook House
1 Lower Ladyes Hills
Kenilworth
Warks CV8 2GN

Dog World
Dog World Ltd
9 Tufton Street
Ashford
Kent TN23 1QN
Tel: 0233 621877

Our Dogs
Our Dogs Publishing Co Ltd
5 Oxford Road Station Approach
Manchester M60 1SX
Tel: 061 236 2660

Pet Plan
Pet Plan House
10-13 Heathfield Terrace
Chiswick
London W4 4JE
Tel: 081 995 1414

FURTHER READING

Juliette de Bairacli Levy
The Complete Herbal Book for the Dog
(Faber, 1975)

John Bleby and Gerald Bishop
The Dog's Health from A to Z
(David & Charles, 1986)

David Coffey MRCVS
A Veterinary Surgeon's Guide to Dogs
(World's Work, 1980)

Andrew Edney
Dog and Cat Nutrition
(Pergamon Press, 1982)

J. Evans & Kay White
The Doglopaedia
(Hemston, 1985)

Eleanor Frankling & Trevor Turner
Practical Dog Breeding and Genetics
(Popular Dogs)

Hancock MRCVS
The Right Way to Keep Dogs
(Elliot, 1975)

Tom Horner
Take Them Round Please
(David & Charles, 1975)

P. R. A. Moxon
Gundogs: Training & Field Trials
(Popular Dogs, 1978)

Kay White
Choose and Bring Up Your Puppy
(Elliot, 1975)

Kay White
Dog Breeding
(Bartholomew, 1984)

Kay White & J. Evans
How to Have a Well-mannered Dog
(Elliot, 1983)

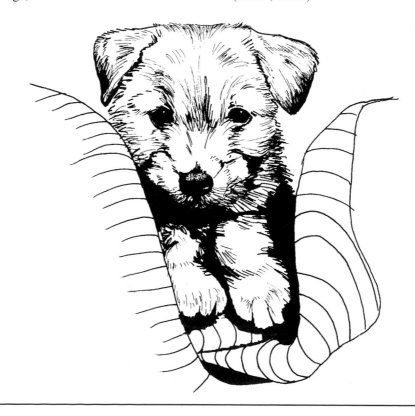

ACKNOWLEDGEMENTS

Heartfelt thanks from The Dogs Home Battersea
to all the contributors to A Passion for Dogs.

To Katie Boyle, HRH Prince Michael of Kent and Desmond Morris.

To Gerald Bishop for 'Making the Most of Your Dog', 'The New Dog or Puppy', 'Feeding, Diet and Nutrition', 'Grooming', 'Breeding', 'The Sick, Injured or Elderly Dog' and 'A-Z of Dog Ailments'; also for many extracts taken from *The Dog's Health A-Z* written by Gerald Bishop and John Bleby (published by David & Charles).

To Sheila Alcock and Les Crawley for 'Rescue', Iain Gordon for 'Working Dogs', T.G. Field-Fisher QC for 'The Dog and The Law', Sheila Zabawa for 'Choosing a Boarding Kennel', Lesley Scott-Ordish for the extract from her book *Heroic Dogs* (Arlington Books, 1990), John A. Rohrbach for 'Complementary Medicine for Dogs' and Wendy Boorer for 'Dogs in Ancient Civilisations', 'Medieval Dogs' and various smaller pieces.

To Janet Pound for 'The Beauty Contest', 'Emma and Kate', 'Play Safe', 'Your Dog's Family Tree' and various smaller pieces. To David Cavill for 'Dog Shows', 'The Kennel Club' and 'Crufts'. To Dee Woodcock for 'Dog Types'.

To Eric Delderfield for 'Dusky', 'Three Faithful Collies', 'Can a Dog Sympathise?'

and 'Cleopatra, Phone Fanatic'.
To Jilly Cooper for 'Rats – The Dog Soldier', 'Bobby of Maiwand', 'Prince – The Miracle Worker' and other smaller pieces. To Sheila Alcock for 'The Challenge'. Corey Ford for 'Every Dog should own a Man', and James Herriot for 'Old Friends'. To Gloria Cottesloe for extracts from her book *The Story of The Dogs Home Battersea*.

To The People's Dispensary for Sick Animals for 'Training the Young Dog', 'Dogs and Holidays' and 'Pets in Summer'. To Pedigree Petfoods for 'Pets for Therapy', 'Puppy Training with Phil Drabble', 'Dogs in the Countryside' and 'The Country Code for Dogs'.

To Paula Rees for the line drawings.

To Marc Henrie for 'Photographing Dogs' and for the majority of the photographs, often specially taken.

To Freddie Reed for permission to use photographs from *A Friend in Need*.

Lastly, to all the employees, former employees and friends of The Dogs Home who have helped in any way with material – especially to those people who have given Battersea dogs happy homes and written to tell us about them.

INDEX

Page numbers in italic denote illustrations.

There is sorrow enough in the natural way
From men and women to fill our day;
But when we are certain of sorrow in store,
Why do we always arrange for more?
Brothers and Sisters, I bid you beware
Of giving your heart to a dog to tear.

Rudyard Kipling